THE BURDEN OF BETRAYAL

The Burden of Betrayal

Non-Offending Priests and the Clergy Child Sexual Abuse Scandals

BARRY O'SULLIVAN

GRACEWING

First published in 2018 by
Gracewing
2 Southern Avenue
Leominster
Herefordshire HR6 0QF
United Kingdom
www.gracewing.co.uk

ISBN 978 085244 841 0

Typeset by Gracewing

Cover design by Bernardita Peña Hurtado

Cover photo credit: Statue of Saint Marcellin Champagnat by Jiménez Deredia, placed opposite the front door of Domus Sanctae Marthae, the papal residence, in The Vatican, Rome, on 20 September 2000. Photograph courtesy of the Archive of the General House of the Marist Brothers and used by permission of the Marist Brothers.

CONTENTS

ACKNOWLEDGEMENTS

I AM INDEBTED TO a number of people without whose help and support my research and this book would not have been completed. I would particularly like to thank the following: Dr Liz Ballinger, my Principal Supervisor at the University of Manchester, for her untiring support and encouragement; and Dr William West, my Secondary Supervisor, for all his useful help and advice.

I would also like to acknowledge my friend and colleague Brother Brendan Geary for his invaluable patience and guidance through some very complex issues.

My gratitude goes to the Bishop and Diocese of Salford for supporting me throughout my research. This support was instrumental in enabling me to begin the research and then to continue it through to completion.

I am pleased as well to acknowledge the gracious and indispensable help offered me by the team at Gracewing publishing, the editorial assistance provided by Andrew Imlach and the clerical assistance furnished by Pam Jones and Catherine Grundy.

Finally, I am especially grateful to the six non-offending priests who gave so generously of their experiences and their most personal insights into a crisis that has challenged our lives and our Church.

Revd Dr Barry O'Sullivan

FOREWORD

In the 1990s I was appointed by the Catholic Bishops' Conference of England and Wales to chair a study group to examine clerical sexual abuse and formulate a response to people who were coming forward and making allegations about child sexual abuse by some priests and religious. This was a tragic situation and one which the Church initially found very difficult to respond to: it was too sensitive and complex to be dealt with comfortably. As the trauma of sex abuse was revealed by victims and survivors so it rippled through their families and communities and society in general. In a sense no one was outside the trauma of abuse. Just as families and communities were divided in their response, so too the Church struggled to understand and reconcile the divisions within and provide a safe space in which to counter this evil.

This book opens up one aspect of the hurt and difficulty within the Church in relation to clerical sexual abuse. Priests were the normal leaders within a Catholic community, but it was a small number of priests who had damaged this community by their abusive behaviour toward children and young adults. The norm had become suspect and ineffective in the eyes of many.

Also in the 1990s I served as the Catholic liaison bishop to the Prison Service and among the body of Catholic prison chaplains I met a young priest from Salford, Revd Barry O'Sullivan, who was trying to respond to the need to minister to priests who were in prison for sexual offences. He had become involved with the rehabilitation programmes provided within the Prison Service to try to understand the behaviour of sex offenders. In 1997 I became the Bishop of Salford and worked with Revd

O'Sullivan to develop a way forward for our diocese. He became the child protection coordinator for the diocese and won the trust and respect of many whom he served in this work, not least his brother priests. His experiences in this ministry led him to undertake research on the effect of the criminal actions of some of their brother priests on their own lives and ministry. This book gives you the opportunity to read this story.

✠ Terence J. Brain
Emeritus Bishop of Salford

INTRODUCTION

ARCHBISHOP MARK COLERIDGE, then Archbishop of Canberra and Goulburn and now Archbishop of Brisbane, wrote in a pastoral letter to the people of his diocese that the 'story of the sexual abuse of the young within the Catholic Church has been the greatest drama of my thirty-six years of priesthood.'[1] The drama of child abuse has not lessened with time. Indeed, there has been increased public awareness of the sexual abuse of children as a result of revelations of abuse by celebrities, in the world of sport, and in towns like Rochdale, Oxford, and Rotherham.[2] The crisis continues for the Catholic Church, with government-led inquiries in Australia, England and Wales, and Scotland, and revelations of the sexual abuse of children in other countries.

As the scandal surrounding this issue has developed, there has been a growing awareness of the number of people who are affected by an allegation of abuse, and the cumulative effect of such allegations on different groups. Revd Dr Barry O'Sullivan points out in this book that growing awareness of sexual abuse led to concern for victims, and of the need to develop policies and protocols to do what was possible to prevent the abuse of children in the future, and to ensure that those who made allegations would be heard and given appropriate support when they came forward. There was also the realization of the need for formation and training for those who were involved in responding to allegations, and of the importance of identifying the specific responsibilities and roles of those who were involved in any way.

There was also concern about how to treat those who had abused. Treatment of sex offenders is a specialized area and there have been significant developments in

recent years. The Church has benefited from these developments and it is now possible to provide specialized
treatment—certainly in the English-speaking world—for
those who have abused.

Archbishop Coleridge's Pastoral Letter was entitled
'Seeing the faces, hearing the voices'. Fortunately, the voices
of victims of abuse are now being heard. Those who perpetrated abuse can explore what led them to abuse children
as part of their therapy. There has been a growing realization, however, that there is an ever-widening circle of people
affected by abuse whose voices are not always heard. This
group is sometimes referred to as 'secondary victims'[3] and
this includes the family members of victims and perpetrators
of abuse, the parish or school where an abuser worked,
parishioners, especially those, for example, who have mem-
ories of special moments in their lives, like weddings, First
Communions, funerals, or bereavements, which now may
appear tainted in some way after revelations of abuse.

Another group which is often overlooked, and whose
'faces are not seen', is the ordinary priests or colleagues of
abusers. As Revd O'Sullivan demonstrates in his research,
this group has also been affected significantly by the fall-out
from the crisis. Ordinary priests and brothers are in the front
line in parishes, schools, and pastoral centres, and often find
themselves involved in conversations about the crisis. As
well as being expected to speak on behalf of the Church, they
are also victims of the crisis, as their own lives have been
deeply affected and changed in many ways. The freedom
they once had to conduct their ministry with confidence and
creativity is now subject to protocols and regulations, not
least the requirement for criminal background checks. This
involves a level of scrutiny and intrusiveness that was not
part of their ministry before the crisis. Revd O'Sullivan's
research shows that the priests accept the necessity of

protocols et cetera, but also that their sense of priesthood, identity and ministry has been affected by the crisis.

Over the past fifteen years I have worked as a therapist with victims of abuse, with perpetrators, with mothers of victims, as a teacher, researcher, writer, and workshop presenter. I have also been involved in preparing guidelines for safeguarding documents. The most difficult role I have undertaken has been as a provincial in my own religious order,[4] where I have tried to balance the claims and expectations of those who make allegations of abuse, with the rights of those who are accused, especially if they are deceased. I have also spoken to each brother in the province about the allegations of abuse and have been moved when I saw the reaction of many brothers who were never involved in abuse and how these revelations affected them personally. One member of the order said that the phrase 'secondary victim' provided a valuable label to help him to name his experience.

Revd O'Sullivan explores in detail the ways in which ordinary priests have been affected by the crisis. In the chapters that follow, he shows that some experienced an existential crisis partly as a result of the changed perception of priests in society, the questions that were raised regarding the behaviour of some of their colleagues and the response of some bishops and religious superiors. We need to recognize that in a globalised world the failures and shortcomings of bishops in other countries have a direct effect on morale as the international nature of the crisis affects priests and religious in every country. The priests who were interviewed experienced grief and loss, feelings of anxiety and fear, a sense of betrayal by brother priests—some of whom they knew personally—and, at an organisational level, by the bishops and the Vatican. Some spoke of being traumatized by the experience.

What is perhaps surprising is that this research has revealed an untold 'good news' story about the fidelity and resilience of the ordinary priests who continue to undertake their pastoral responsibilities with commitment and sensitivity to the needs of their parishioners and students. This confirms research undertaken by others that priests often feel stressed by their work, but also experience satisfaction in their ministry. The abuse crisis has been difficult for them individually, in their ministry, and in their confidence in Church leadership and organisational structures; but it does not appear to have undermined their sense of the worth of their pastoral ministry. It is worth noting that those who were interviewed said that the experience of the interview was the first opportunity they had had to reflect on and discuss this issue at depth with another priest.

Revd O'Sullivan's research highlights the importance of dialogue and communication, and the need to provide training in this area for priests and, where necessary, to provide facilitators who can enable good communication to take place. This may involve a dialogue between a priest and his bishop, or between a bishop and his presbyterate, as it is often important for the priests to meet as a group with their bishops to create dialogue and a listening space regarding matters of shared concern. Avoidance of such meetings due to fear or lack of skills only creates a sense of disappointment, disillusionment, of not being valued, or of not being taken into account by those in authority, who also have a duty of care to the men who have promised obedience as part of their priestly life.

This research, as does Revd O'Sullivan's current research project to interview bishops to understand their experience of dealing with the abuse crisis, enables voices to be heard from other participants in the drama of the sexual abuse of children by clergy and religious brothers.

In doing so, Revd O'Sullivan has done a significant service to ordinary priests as well as to bishops as these research projects help us to understand better how leadership engages with priests, and they can help priests to understand the responses of bishops who had no preparation for the crisis that confronted them.

Hopefully the voices of other people affected by this crisis will also be heard. Such research and opportunities for dialogue enable the truth to be shared and to set us free (Jn 8:32). It can also contribute to understanding and healing as we learn from the mistakes and hurts of the past and move to a situation where safeguarding is seen as a necessary and valued part of Church life, for the protection of children and the well-being of those in ministry.

Brother Brendan Geary, FMS
Provincial of the Marist Brothers' Province of West Central
Europe
HCPC Registered Clinical Psychologist

Notes

[1] M. B. Coleridge, *Seeing the Faces, Hearing the Voices* (Catholic Diocese of Wollongong, 2010).

[2] B. Geary, 'Child sexual abuse' in *The Christian Handbook of Abuse, Addiction and Difficult Behaviour* (revised and expanded edition) (Stowmarket, SFK, UK: Kevin Mayhew, in press).

[3] G. Fieldhouse Byrne, 'The voices of secondary victims of clergy sexual abuse' in *The Dark Night of the Catholic Church* (Stowmarket, SFK, UK: Kevin Mayhew, 2011), pp. 279–298.

[4] Brother Geary is the provincial (superior) of the Marist Brothers' province of West Central Europe, which comprises Ireland, the United Kingdom, the Netherlands, Belgium and Germany. He was appointed as the provincial in December 2009.

1

THE SCANDALS AND NON-OFFENDING PRIESTS

Starting the journey

'IT'S THE WORST thing that has ever happened to me as a priest,' admitted Matthew as we sat together in his presbytery in southeast England. 'I feel absolutely drained by this.'

I had known Matthew for scarcely two hours. I had arrived in the late morning for our scheduled interview, we had had a quick lunch together and he had shown me his church, a medium-sized urban church typical of many built in the 1960s. He knew only that I was a brother priest who was researching the impact of the sexual abuse of children by some priests in the Catholic Church; yet he was willing to share with me his very personal struggle to make sense of what he admitted was his most painful experience in three decades as a priest. In truth, Matthew was actually very much more than just willing to share.

I had wondered on the train from Manchester whether he would talk at all about this most difficult subject for any priest. I had embarked on a doctoral study which called for individual interviews with six non-offending priests from the Church's twenty-two dioceses in the Bishops' Conference of England and Wales. Matthew was the first, so I did not know if any of them would reveal their true feelings to me. Would they trust me enough to disclose whether these unthinkable acts of betrayal had affected how they saw themselves, their roles as priests, and their view of our Church following its handling of these scandals over two decades? Would they be comfortable enough to talk at all?

I recalled from my own formation as a priest that Matthew and the other five priests in my study would have been taught to focus outward on the spiritual and emotional ordeals of our parishioners. But I was also learning from my psychological studies and my work for the Church in safeguarding children from abuse that victimhood is a condition that ripples through families and communities, often extending far beyond the primary casualties to reach other groups of victims as well. Would my six priests have encountered this? Would they display signs that the trauma inflicted on children by clergy sex abusers had also affected them? Would they allow themselves to reveal these signs if it had?

When the six were selected by my then University of Manchester academic supervisor, Dr William West, they had been assured that their identities would be known only to me. 'Matthew' is therefore not his real name. To preserve their anonymity and their privacy, I refer to Matthew and his five brother priests by pseudonyms I have given them. But while their names are not real, their feelings are very real, and very personal. Would they be able to articulate them? Would they be willing to speak on the record, even with their true identities withheld?

I was also worried about my own role as the researcher, especially as I was what in academic terminology is known as an 'insider researcher', in my case a priest researching fellow priests and the practices of our Church. Would I lead the interview too much instead of allowing Matthew and his colleagues to share their thoughts and experiences unimpeded by my desire for rich data? As I listened to Matthew, my worries began to fade.

Sitting securely in his church, he revealed that this was his first meaningful, mature conversation about the clergy child sex abuse cases and their impact on him and on the Church. He had touched on the subject previously in casual conversations with brother priests; but he confessed that these conversations had never progressed beyond the 'urban myths' of priests and their vulnerability to false allegations. This was something I had also encountered during my work for the Church in safeguarding children and vulnerable adults.

Matthew spoke openly and at length to me about the effects he felt from the scandals, seeming to appreciate the opportunity to talk about them. I asked my questions but didn't need to break the ice; there were no uncomfortable pauses or awkward silences. He talked, and kept talking, something I was also to find in each of my five subsequent interviews.

To my knowledge, Matthew and his five brother priests had never been accused of any wrongdoing. But Matthew disclosed to me that he knew a priest who had been imprisoned for child sex abuse and this disturbed him deeply, perhaps even more deeply than he realised himself. Another priest I was to interview, Philip, told me that he had met victims of abuse and a third, Daniel, recounted how he had replaced a priest who had been convicted. All had seen the effects of the scandals ripple throughout the Catholic world.

As I left Matthew I felt greatly encouraged. If the other five interviewees were as forthcoming as he had been, this would be a very revealing study into the psychological effects of the scandals on non-offending priests as a perhaps less obvious group of victims. It would also reveal how the Church's handling of the scandals affected their views on the Catholic Church as our font of spiritual, moral, and intellectual wisdom, our employer and our life.

'Giving your life, that's what this is all about,' said Matthew.

A double scandal

In the course of my work as a priest in the Catholic Church in England and Wales, and especially as one of the Church's specialists in the field of safeguarding children, I have experienced first-hand the extensive controversy generated by cases of the sexual abuse of children by some Catholic priests and, more broadly, by others in society at large. These cases from around the Catholic world and investigations into them by the media and official organisations have led to numerous official Church and various governments' reports and policy statements, pronouncements by leaders of the Catholic Church and of other faiths, as well as many books, articles, and academic theses. This controversy, as many authors have pointed out, has subdivided the subject of sexual abuse by clerics into two dimensions: the fact that the abuse occurred at all, and the way the problem was managed once it came to light.

This controversy has focused mainly on the trauma of the children who were the primary victims of abuse, and on the effects on the Church as a religious institution. This is of course legitimate considering the unthinkable betrayal of these children by the offending clerics and, it has often been argued, the almost equally unthinkable betrayal of the children, the Church, and its principles by some bishops and religious superiors in senior leadership positions in the Catholic Church which has been widely criticized for mishandling the allegations and the perpetrators.

There have also been analyses of offending priests. A study in 2000 by T. W. Haywood and J. Green, for example, sought to explore the similarities with and differences between clerics who sexually abuse and other sex offenders. They reported that clerics were generally older and better educated, and that 77 per cent of accused clerics had been accused by male victims compared with 46 per cent for other groups in society.[1]

While the children who were abused are the primary victims and therefore rightly remain the primary concern, there are also impacts on a number of what American psychoanalyst and pastoral educator Dr Joanne Marie Greer, among others, calls 'secondary victims'[2] who are affected by the fallout when abuse has taken place. In the context of the sexual abuse crisis within the Catholic Church, Dr Greer, a child abuse specialist and Professor Emerita of Pastoral Counselling at Loyola University in Maryland, states that 'secondary victim' describes a Catholic distressed by the child sexual abuse crisis among the clergy. He or she is 'a person who has emotional and practical ties to the perpetrator by blood, marriage, friendship, or colleagueship, or church membership'. The perpetrator's actions have a negative effect on the secondary victim's life.

She notes this phenomenon has been recognised only recently as studies, including those related to other crimes, identify that the beliefs and standards of secondary victims are shaken so they can, for example, misdirect blame and responsibility, become resentful and, in the case of non-offending priests, they can start to question their preparation for ministry.

She offers an extensive list of secondary victims of the clergy offender: the present and future families of the abused child; the child's friends; the family of the abuser; parishioners; and the wider Catholic community. Dr Greer also lists particular categories of innocent priests: the offender's

religious order; brother priests and superiors; those to whom
he ministered in the past; and those to whom he ministered
concurrent with the abuse. To this could be added the
Church's bishops and religious leaders, the clergy of other
religions, and those in other professions which either deal
with children or whose occupations are also facing abuse
allegations. While not guilty of any misdeed, it seems that
they all have to endure guilt by association.

There has been some acknowledgement of the effects
of this scandal on one group of secondary victims: parishioners whose faith in the Church could have been shaken.
For example, Mary, a parishioner from a Catholic parish
in the north of England, said:

> My emotional and physical world was turned
> upside down. I loved the Church and had brought
> my own family up to respect her and look to her
> for guidance and support. As a teacher I taught the
> children to seek out priests when times were hard.
> All I could feel at this time was a deep sense of
> betrayal—tears for the children who were abused
> and most of all tears for my Church.[3]

And another parishioner, Phil, added:

> I found myself asking: 'How could this happen in
> God's true Church?' If my Christianity wasn't
> damaged, my satisfaction with the Catholic Church
> certainly was. I had taken a radical step in convert-
> ing to Catholicism and it was difficult not to feel
> thoroughly let down.[4]

However, aside from Dr Greer's identification of the secondary victim effects on some clergy, very little attention
has been paid to non-offending priests in general. There
have been some published views of individual innocent
priests and in 2011 Msgr Dr S. J. Rossetti, an American
psychologist and professor of pastoral studies, published

the results of a general survey he conducted of almost 2,500 priests in the United States which, among many other things, found them to be happy in their work.[5] But no extensive data has been collected and interpreted to determine whether there are psychological and ontological effects (in terms of identity) from the Church's child sex abuse scandals which are felt by priests who have played no part in any of these cases other than to attempt to continue their vocation while besieged by accusations and controversy. This gap in the otherwise extensive collection of information and opinion on the scandals met my university's research criteria which required me to conduct intense research into a narrow and therefore manageable subject area. Rather than examining all of the secondary victims, I could therefore focus on the one group of secondary victims I knew best, a group which had been—and to a great extent is still being—overlooked and, indeed, a group that would not think of themselves as victims even if I was to find evidence that this is just what they are.

I was therefore convinced of the importance of identifying and analysing the effects on non-offending Catholic priests in England and Wales through in-depth interviews with a representative sample of six of them. Six out of a clergy of nearly 5,900 may not seem to be many, and for a quantitative study it would not be. However, for a qualitative study seeking to probe deeply rather than broadly, six is a sample size in accordance with the guidance of the founder of interpretative phenomenological analysis (IPA), the qualitative psychological research methodology with which I was familiar through my non-religious training to become a qualified counsellor and therapist. I conducted these interviews as strictly controlled research for a professional doctorate from the University of Manchester.

In this book, 'non-offending' refers to priests who have not been accused of inappropriate sexual behaviour towards children and, although other faiths have also been affected by such scandals, the 'Church' here refers exclusively to the Catholic Church. While there are many forms of 'abuse' and there have been allegations of other abuses by clergy, I deal here exclusively with the most common and the most widely publicised form of abuse allegations against priests: the sexual abuse of minors under 18 years of age. It has been these cases primarily which have caused the National Catholic Safeguarding Commission (NCSC) to define sexual abuse as:

> Forcing or enticing a child or young person to take part in sexual activities, including prostitution, whether or not the child is aware of what is happening. For vulnerable adults, it is activities or acts to which the adult has not consented, or could not consent, or was pressurised into consenting. The activities may include physical contact, including penetrative (*e.g.* rape, buggery, oral sex) or non-penetrative acts. It may also include non-contact activities such as involving children in looking at or in the production of pornographic material, or watching sexual activities, or encouraging children to behave in sexually inappropriate ways. The most common indicator of sexual abuse is the child's disclosure.

The nature and extent of the crisis

In the early 1990s, the scandal of the sexual abuse of children by some members of the clergy emerged as what Mark Dowd, then a BBC Radio 4 religious affairs correspondent, was to describe in a 2010 interview with me as 'the greatest threat to the Catholic Church since the Reformation'. This scandal was compounded by the unsatisfactory initial response by those responsible for addressing the crisis: the Catholic hierarchy, bishops, and major superiors of religious orders. The issue was especially sensitive given that the sexual abuse of minors is such a taboo subject within the Catholic Church.

The Catholic Safeguarding Advisory Service (CSAS) records that from 2003 to 2012 there were 598 allegations of all types of abuses reported to statutory authorities by the Church's dioceses and religious institutes in England and Wales. These cases ranged from a low of forty-one in each of 2006 and 2009 to a high of 100 in 2004 and were spread across all the dioceses of England and Wales. In total, 465 (77 per cent) of these cases were allegations of sexual abuse. Of the total number of allegations, 487 arose from diocesan contexts and 111 from religious contexts. For clarification, a diocesan priest belongs to a geographical area, such as my own Salford Diocese, and a religious priest belongs to a religious order, such as the Benedictines or the Franciscans, and belongs to a province, such as England and Wales.

In March 2014, an independent review was commissioned by the National Catholic Safeguarding Commission (NCSC). The following statistics are taken from the independent review, which was led by Dr Stephen Bullivant. The review researched the allegation statistics for the Catholic Church in England and Wales between 2003 and 2012. It reported that priests constituted the largest group of the Church's alleged offenders, making up nearly 60 per cent of the allegations. The percentage of abuse allegations against diocesan priests (39.96 per cent) was more than double that of allegations against priests from a religious order (18.37 per cent). To my knowledge, there is no data to explain why allegations against diocesan priests are considerably more common that those priests from a religious order. Nearly seven per cent of all allegations were against nuns, while the rest of the allegations were against Church lay employees or volunteers.

There were at least 425 alleged clergy child sex abusers reported in official figures. Fifty-two laicisations (permanent removal from priestly office) were completed between 2001 and 2013 in England and Wales as a direct result of abuse.

Whilst sexual abuse is by far the most common form of alleged abuse, physical abuse (13 per cent), emotional abuse (5 per cent), and child abusive images (5 per cent) should be noted lest they be forgotten and reduced to the shadows of sexual molestation of children by the clergy. These cases did not, however, lead to such intense public attention directed at the clergy and were not covered in my study.

The sense of shock and betrayal which can be heard from bishops and priests who have been affected by the sexual abuse crisis is compounded by the fact that these offences were perpetrated by a few among the thousands of priests and permanent deacons in the twenty-two dioceses of England and Wales who serve an estimated Catholic population of over four million. The alleged abusers were people whose vocation was directed to the pastoral care and service of others, particularly the most vulnerable in society.

Child protection policies and the perception of priests from a Catholic diocese in the north of England

Allegations of the abuse of minors by priests led the Catholic Church in England and Wales to establish procedures and structures to ensure the safeguarding of children. I therefore began to examine the effects of the abuse scandals on non-offending priests in 2007 by researching the views of hundreds of priests from a diocese in the north of England on how they felt about these new protection measures (the full results of this research can be found in the Appendix to this book). The research was conducted by a written questionnaire to which the priests replied anonymously, enabling them to be as candid as they wished. Here are some of the responses to two of the seven questions.

> Question: If you found yourself the subject of an allegation, are you confident that the Child Protection Commission would treat you fairly and with respect?

A total of 43 per cent of the priests reported that they were confident they would be treated properly, while 26 per cent were unsure and another 17 per cent did not know. Fourteen per cent did not think they would receive a fair hearing.

But one priest wrote: 'Once falsely accused, a priest could never prove his innocence.' Another priest offered the following:

> I'm not sure I would have answered question 6 so positively if I was not aware of how the commission has dealt with someone I know. I would probably have opted for 'not sure' or 'don't know'—so if these are the main responses to that question it is probably because most people have not had any direct dealings with the commission.

Another respondent wrote:

> All animals are equal. Some are more equal than others. While the so-called paramountcy principle [the interests of a child are always paramount] is maintained, justice will never happen or be seen to happen. It conflicts with the human rights of clergy and defies canon law. It is also possibly illegal as it discriminates on the ground of age.

I asked the following question:

> Has the adoption of child protection policies and
> procedures given you confidence to continue your
> ministry with children and vulnerable adults?

While 54 per cent of the priests expressed confidence in
the Church's safeguarding policies and procedures, 38 per
cent were not sure and 6 per cent did not know. Eight per
cent did not feel confident in continuing to minister to
children and vulnerable adults.

Among the written responses were the following:

> Credence must rightly be given to children—no
> problem—but not at the expense of denying other
> persons respect of their rights.

> Two wrongs do not make a right. Not to listen to
> a child is wrong—and we need to create the situa-
> tion where a child can freely speak knowing he or
> she will be listened to.

These responses indicate the struggle non-offending
priests were having with concerns about the imbalance
and injustice about the response to the allegations both as
a Church and as a society.

According to feedback from safeguarding training
which I facilitated with ninety-six Catholic priests in 2011,
the prevailing anxiety amongst the vast majority of priests
seemed to be the possibility of a malicious allegation. This
observation is also based on my experience of being a
diocesan safeguarding co-ordinator for eleven years,
during which time it was the only anxiety that was voiced
during both group and individual interviews with priests.
This anxiety seemed to be at the root of the marked
decline I have noted in the provision of pastoral care to
children.

The need to conduct in-depth research

To investigate in more detail the effects of the scandals on non-offending priests, I was initially faced with the challenge of trying to capture the experience of almost 5,900 Catholic priests working across England and Wales. The Bishops' Conferences of Scotland and of Ireland (including Northern Ireland) are separate conferences, hence the limitation to priests ministering in England and Wales. But even with this limitation, adopting a quantitative approach would make it difficult to reach conclusions with any certainty, given the size of the cohort and the lack to date of Church discussion about the effects on non-offending priests.

The task would be even more difficult because the priests had not discussed their personal perspectives on the issue before and my research would focus on the taboo subjects of the sexual abuse of children and the role of their Church. Further complicating matters was the fact that many cases occurring elsewhere in the Catholic world had been widely reported in England and Wales, as had been responses from Church leaders, including Popes and other senior officials in the Vatican. It was therefore imperative to select the methodologies that would best handle the situation, so I chose a qualitative method because I considered it would be the most appropriate way of investigating the complexity of the sensitive issues involved.

I decided to conduct personal interviews with non-offending priests to explore the effects on their psychological, emotional, and spiritual lives as a result of the abuses by some brother priests both domestically and globally. I would also explore the effects of the scandals on non-offending priests and their day-to-day ministry with children and examine the effects on the institutional relationship of all priests with the Catholic Church, its hierarchy, and procedures, both in a spiritual and moral sense and as their trainer and employer. This, again, is at least in part because the scandal of clergy child sexual abuse is widely regarded as leading to a second scandal for the Church caused by its initial handling of abuse allegations,[6] something I have seen as a former church safeguarding co-ordinator. Non-offending priests could be regarded as secondary victims in this aspect of the scandals as well.

Following the recommendations of leaders in the field of psychological research,[7] I opted for a qualitative research tool to capture 'in-depth portraits' of the individual experiences of six randomly selected priests whom I would interview. I chose interpretative phenomenological analysis (IPA) as my qualitative method and hermeneutic phenomenological methodology as the most appropriate and effective way to elicit the data which I wished to investigate, as hermeneutics is the methods used to interpret language, especially biblical language. IPA is an approach to qualitative research that examines people's detailed personal lived experiences to see how they make sense of their lives in the context in which they live. I assumed IPA would suit the philosophical and theological formation of my interviewees. However, I could not know for sure until I tested it. I was especially interested in whether IPA was appropriate or even possible when applied to research with fellow Catholic priests to glean some insight into how their experience of fellow clergy committing such atrocious acts had impacted on, or been assimilated into, their world view.

Finding a balance between psychology, sociology and theology was one of the most difficult tasks I faced, particularly for me as an 'insider researcher'. Swinton and Mowat of the University of Aberdeen have noted that practical theology is valuable in considering critically and theologically the interaction of the practices of the Church with the practices of the rest of the world:

> Practical theology seeks to reveal and reflect on the intricate, diverse but complementary meanings of Christian practices and to enable faithful presence and action.[8]

In general, phenomenological research seeks to clarify experiences from a person's everyday life. As such, phenomenology strives to be as true as possible to the phenomenon and the context of its occurrence in the world of the interviewee. My aim was to capture as closely as possible the first-hand accounts of my interviewees and the way in which the phenomenon was experienced by them.

IPA is an approach to qualitative research that examines people's detailed personal lived experiences to see how they make sense of their lives in the context in which they live. This context is sharply focused on their lived experience of the topic. IPA tries to understand the world from the participant's perspective, mediated by the context of cultural and social historical meaning. Thus, the process of making sense of the participants' experience is inevitably interpretive and the role of the researcher in making sense of the participant's account is affected by the researcher's own pre-conceptions.

By choosing IPA for my research methodology I committed myself to exploring, interpreting and situating the means by which my selected priests made sense of their experience of this especially testing topic. I was required to concentrate on interpreting accurately and faithfully the experiences they related to me, with the hermeneutic of suspicion, a method of interpretation that does not take motives at face value.

> In order to understand what is actually going on
> within that situation it is necessary to understand
> the meaning of the actions, the way the situation
> is being interpreted by those performing within it
> and the reasons behind the ways individuals and
> communities act in the particular ways that they
> do. The quest for this type of understanding forms
> the heart of qualitative research and is a fundamen-
> tal dimension of practical theology's endeavour to
> critically reflect on the nature of situation.[9]

As a researcher, I did not find IPA an easy option but was attracted to it for its accessibility, flexibility and applicability. I found it especially useful in my attempts to capture the lived world of my interviewees with regard to extraordinarily challenging issues. Whilst I tried to observe and capture 'a person in context' in their meaningful world, I was aware I could never fully escape the preconceptions that I brought to the research from my own world and experience.

As the researcher, I found the process bidirectional as each of my six priests and I made a significant effort to immerse ourselves into the process. I found this to be especially pronounced given my stance as an 'insider researcher'. Success as a phenomenological researcher did not ultimately depend upon my revealing an interviewee's 'pure' experience: it was dependent upon my reporting the most sensitive and accurate account I could.

An insider researcher

My background, both personal and professional, related to the subject at many points. My background gave me special access to and an insight into the views of non-offending priests.

I was ordained a Catholic priest on 18 July 1987. I have been a priest, based in the Diocese of Salford, for three decades. For eleven years, I was the diocesan child protection (now safeguarding) co-ordinator. It is the responsibility of the diocesan safeguarding co-ordinator to oversee and implement the agreed safeguarding policies and procedures of the Church in England and Wales, working, as always, within the legal requirements, national and canonical, as they have been developed in recent years. The diocesan safeguarding co-ordinator is responsible for responding to any concerns with regards to clergy and other personnel, both employed and voluntary.

From 1995 to 1999, I was the Chaplain at HMP Wymott, where I was also a tutor for the Prison Service's Sex Offender Treatment Programme. From 1999 to 2001, I studied in Boston, USA, and obtained a Master's degree in Counselling Psychology. I then returned to the Diocese of Salford to be its safeguarding co-ordinator until 2012. During that time, I obtained a Postgraduate Certificate in Behavioural Forensic Psychology from the University of Central Lancashire in 2010 and became a Member of the Child Exploitation Online Protection (CEOP) Academy. From 2007 to 2012, I was an *Ex-Officio* Member of the Anglophone Conference for Safeguarding at Vatican City. I am a Member of the British Association for Counselling and Psychotherapy (BACP).

As a practising therapist and as a Catholic priest, I have been in an unusual position of counselling both clergy perpetrators of child sexual abuse and the primary victims of such abuse. I was both concerned and disappointed that the victims all too often reported a woefully inadequate response from Church authorities to their accusations, a response which often included accusations of lying and seeking compensation. Ironically, the clergy perpetrators who were my clients more often than not reported a sense of being abandoned by their religious superior.

'Insider research' refers to situations when researchers themselves belong to the populations being studied. The researcher shares an identity and experiential base with the interviewees. 'Insider' is defined as an individual who possesses *a priori* intimate knowledge of the community and its members' views.

This can be advantageous as it may allow researchers quicker and more complete acceptance by their participants. It can be argued that participants will be more open with researchers whose commonality can be a basis of mutual trust. However, experts in this field point out that being an 'insider' can potentially cause problems.[10] Researchers might experience role conflict if they find themselves caught between 'loyalty tugs'[11] or in role confusion, for example when a researcher answers participants or analyses data as an insider rather than as a researcher.

As an insider researcher interviewing fellow Catholic priests, I assumed I would be perceived principally as a brother priest and this turned out to be the case, although this was not a term any of the interviewees used. That relationship of brother priests automatically created a particular dynamic between each of my interviewees and me. The complexities of this dynamic are explored further later in this book. This dynamic also gave rise to another consideration, given my previous role within the Catholic Church as a diocesan safeguarding co-ordinator. I knew that, whilst I saw my safeguarding role as promoting the Church's safeguarding policies and procedures as spelled out in 2001 by the Church's Nolan Committee, there was every likelihood that I would be perceived by the interviewees as a person who was responsible, along with the statutory authorities, for investigating allegations and disclosures. Thus I was potentially an insider researcher in two ways: first as a fellow priest and secondly as someone intimately bound up in the area of experience I was asking my interviewees to share with me.

Another tension that arose for me was that between theology and psychology. Fr Jim Christie, SJ, a priest who has been a psychotherapist for over thirty-five years, specifically addresses this tension which he observes in the Catholic Church as a body. He states:

> Meanwhile, all psychological approaches (and everything by Freud in particular) were being viewed by the Church with the deepest suspicion that they were pernicious libertarian nonsense and not worth studying.[12]

In fairness to Fr Christie, he goes on to acknowledge a significant mind shift in recent years on behalf of psychologists and theologians. As a Catholic priest who is also a registered therapist, I found it a tremendous challenge to perform this exercise without attempting to integrate theology into the discussion. The challenge lay in remaining loyal to the clinical purpose of the research, whilst acknowledging and respecting the theological world view of each of the interviewees. The subject was specifically about Catholic priests, about the Catholic Church in England and Wales and about a live crisis in the universal Catholic Church. Whilst the study is principally a clinical one, I felt I could not do it justice without acknowledging and exploring the theological perspectives that the interviewees demonstrated.

As an insider researcher I was conscious of the danger of what might be called an over-rapport with the participants. I was slightly anxious that my overfamiliarity with the world my interviewees inhabited might be perceived by others as leading to a lack of objectivity which could foster torn loyalties. Whilst over-rapport is a common criticism of insider researchers, this can be an advantage, given the nature of religious knowledge and the role of faith in the work of the clergy interviewees.

The particular Catholic context meant that, as an insider in this community, I could best access and understand the thoughts, feelings and experiences of the clergy participants. The complexity of this dynamic required a degree of insider status to enable me as the researcher to engage in meaningful conversation with fellow clergy members about their experience, especially given the sensitive topic. It is my belief that the advantages of an insider perspective far outweighed any potentially adverse effects of over-rapport. As American researcher Dr Claire Robertson observes: 'The collection of life stories cannot be done well without first acquiring a thorough knowledge of the culture or subculture in which one is working.'[13]

As a fellow Catholic priest and an insider researcher, I found Dr Robertson's observations echoed my own experiences whilst interviewing the participants. Dr Robertson puts it succinctly:

> It was advantageous to our communication that the researcher had had a theological education. We could use 'shortcut terminology' and still have mutual understanding ... Our rapport was such that I don't recall moments when there was a lack of understanding or misunderstanding that was not cleared up by subsequent questions.[14]

I found it valuable to research my peers in settings familiar to them (their place of work/home) as it afforded me enhanced rapport with the interviewees. Because we came from a 'shared world', the level of engagement was both immediate and rich.

I found bracketing off preconceptions, as far as IPA allows, one of the most challenging aspects of the interviews. I often struggled with my experience, my significant

knowledge of and passion for safeguarding and my affili-
ation with and affection for my brother priests. This
tension was especially testing when I heard them say
things about safeguarding which I knew to be untrue. For
example, a number of interviewees said that any accusation of sexual abuse meant that their ministry was finished.
Not only is this contrary to the Church's national policies
and procedures, but I know that only accusations that have
been sustained have resulted in withdrawal from ministry.
I was torn between being frustrated at their lack of
understanding about such a vital topic and their lack of
training, about which they each expressed concern.

In his 2001 doctoral thesis, 'Sexually offending and
non-offending Catholic priests: characterization and analysis', Fr Dr Gerard J. McGlone, SJ, echoes my own experience of being a priest interviewing brother priests and my
realisation that the depth of engagement by the interviewees was influenced by the fact that I was a fellow priest.
Regarding his research, Fr McGlone wrote:

> Noteworthy in the demographics is the fact that
> 67 per cent of the priest participants in this study
> would not have participated in this research had
> the researcher not been a priest. This is important
> for future researchers to understand, and argues
> that priests need to engage in research. The neces-
> sity of gaining more information about the priest
> population is primary to advancing the field.[15]

For each of the ways that an insider researcher enhances
the understanding of the participants being interviewed,
questions about the objectivity and reflexivity of the
research are raised. I was aware that I perhaps knew too
much about the experience of being a priest in the context
we were exploring and that my own Gestalt was very
similar to those I interviewed. I was also conscious that

there was another way in which I could confuse my roles: not just priest versus researcher, but also safeguarding expert and counsellor versus researcher. There was potential for me to interpret their experiences from my own safeguarding role or from my training as a counsellor.

As a member of the Child Exploitation Online Protection Academy (CEOP) of the United Kingdom National Crime Agency (NCA), I found myself, sometimes consciously and often having reflected on the interview afterwards, having fallen into the trap of 'mining' for information in much the same way as one would during an investigation or risk assessment. On reflection, I have acknowledged in my findings that this dynamic, at least in part, patterned the process. At times, I unintentionally judged the interviewees for some of their responses, something which needed recognising and untangling in supervision.

Overall I believe that acceptance by the group one is studying is one of the significant advantages of this insider research stance. As Fr McGlone found, a common identity can lead to a level of trust and openness in the participants that would probably not have been present otherwise. As a Catholic priest interviewing other priests, I was afforded access to a group that might otherwise be closed to 'outsiders'. All the interviewees were fully aware that I was a fellow Catholic priest, with special responsibility for the subject being researched. The participants seemed to be more willing to discuss their experiences because there was an assumption of mutual understanding and shared distinctiveness, and a feeling that I was 'one of us' and not an outsider who did not understand.

The interview process

From 26 to 29 April 2011 I was part of an organising committee for a national conference entitled 'Safeguarding as Ministry'. The primary purpose of this conference was to explore priests' experience of ministry to children in light of the child sex abuse scandal and the introduction of robust safeguarding policies and procedures. At the conference there was a priest representing each of the twenty-two Catholic dioceses in England and Wales.

I informed the delegates of my intention to do further detailed research about the sexual abuse crisis in the Catholic Church and how this had affected non-offending priests working in England and Wales. The delegates all agreed to be part of a resource bank out of which my then academic supervisor, Dr West, would randomly contact six delegates with the request that they engage in a one-to-one semi-structured interview.

After randomly contacting six delegates, my supervisor informed me of those whom he had chosen and who were willing to be interviewed. After approval was obtained from the University Research Ethics Committee, the interviewees were invited to engage in a one-to-one IPA interview, the process and purpose of which was outlined for them.

Over a six-month period I interviewed each of the six for approximately one hour. Each was asked the following questions:

- Q1. Can you tell me about your journey to becoming a priest?
- Q2. Can you tell me about the experience of being a priest in the shadow of the child abuse scandal?
- Q3. Can you tell me what resources are there to help you in this particular ministry?
- Q4. How do you feel about the training/support you have received in this area?
- Q5. How does your ministry to children compare to when you were first ordained?

- Q6. Have you got a sense of how the policies and procedures adopted by the diocese have affected your ministry with children?
- Q7. How do you think the hierarchy dealt with this issue?
- Q8. Do you have a sense that being a Catholic priest singles you out as somehow different from other denominations/faiths with regard to this issue?

These questions were asked in the context of a semi-structured interview which allowed for certain nuances. All eight questions were covered in each, but the depth of response was largely determined by the interviewees. Out of each interview emerged a unique double hermeneutic which facilitated the opportunity for greater immersion into the data.

Due to the dynamic nature of the interviews, every question did not have to be asked in the same order or exactly the same way. I could therefore determine how a particular question was phrased depending on how the participant was responding. Whilst I could move away from questions on my schedule, consideration also had to be given to how much movement was acceptable. The research questions in IPA focus upon a person's experiences or understandings of particular phenomena in particular contexts. As suggested by Shaw and Flowers at a 2010 conference on IPA I attended at Aston University, all IPA research questions are open, exploratory rather than explanatory, should focus on meaning and sense-making, and are both answerable and worth answering. The primary focus should relate to the experience at hand and my interviewee's understanding of it.

> You may, however, have a secondary question, informed by prior experience, theoretical interest or applied concerns. You cannot guarantee that

you will be able to answer it; but, provided that you remain focused on what your participants can tell you ([that is], are not testing a theory, or making inferences about causality, or 'what happens'), it is fine to set these.[16]

Given that central to IPA is an attempt to enter as deeply as possible into the phenomenological and social world of the participant, I knew that opportunities had to be given for the interviewees to introduce topics which I had not envisaged. The participant should always be regarded as the expert on their own experience with the subject and be given the maximum opportunity to tell their own story as they understand it; this is what I attempted to facilitate. The questions served as a prompt to draw out the appropriate data.

One of the main advantages of a semi-structured interview is that it facilitates rapport, allows for flexibility and enables an interview to go in unexpected directions and, as such, increases the possibility of producing valuable data. In my interviews, the semi-structured approach was important to recognise and explore surprises as they arose. Often an unexpected and hitherto unrecognised reality proved to be the most valuable, precisely because it had been unexpected and, as such, was often particularly important for the interviewee.

To report the experience of the interviewees as faithfully as possible, I attempted to weave the hermeneutics of empathy into the hermeneutic circle which was very evident with each participant. Whilst each priest was trying to make sense of and communicate to me the reality of his world, I was in turn trying to make sense of each priest trying to make sense of his own world, both during each interview and later in analysing the text of each interview.

The dynamic which IPA encourages a researcher to create is dependent, as far as possible, on the interviewer bracketing off preconceptions, resisting the temptation to prejudge and faithfully respecting and recording the account of the participant. With this in mind, on the advice of the University Research Ethics Committee, I had the interviews transcribed by an independent third party.

Notes

[1]   T. W. Haywood and J. Green, 'Cleric serial offenders: Clinical characteristics and treatment approaches' in *Serial Offenders: Current Thought, Recent Findings* (Boca Raton, FL, USA: CRC Press, 2000), pp. 247–262.

[2]   J. M. Greer, 'Secondary victims in a sexual abuse scandal' presentation to the *Safeguarding Children and Young People Conference*, Marist Brothers General House, Rome, March 2012.

[3]   B. Geary and J. M. Greer (eds.), *The Dark Night of the Catholic Church* (Stowmarket, SFK, UK: Kevin Mayhew, 2011), p. 281.

[4]   *Ibid.*, p. 285.

[5]   S. J. Rossetti, *Why Priests are Happy: A Study of the Psychological and Spiritual Health of Priests* (Notre Dame, IN, USA: Ave Maria Press, 2011).

[6]   See, for example: M. Keenan, *Child Sexual Abuse and the Catholic Church: Gender, Power, and Organizational Culture* (New York: Oxford University Press, 2011).

[7]   See, for example: J. A. Smith, et al., *Interpretative Phenomenological Analysis: Theory, Method and Research* (London: Sage, 2009).

[8]   J. Swinton and H. Mowat, *Practical Theology and Qualitative Research* (London: SCM Press. 2006), p. 10.

[9]   *Ibid.*, p. 38.

[10]   P. Adler, et al., *The Oxford Handbook of Sociology, Social Theory and Organization Studies: Contemporary Currents* (Oxford: Oxford University Press, 1990).

[11]   T. Brannick and D. Coghlan, 'In defence of being native: The case for insider academic research' in *Organizational Research Methods*, 10/1 (2007), pp. 59–74.

[12]   J. Christie, 'When theology trumps psychology' in *The Tablet*, 15/February (2014), pp. 14–17.

[13]   C. Robertson, 'In pursuit of life histories: The problem of bias' in

Frontiers: A Journal of Women Studies, 7/2 (1983), p. 84.

[14] *Ibid.,* p. 92.

[15] G. McGlone, *Sexually Offending and Non-Offending Roamn Catholic Priests: Characterization and Analysis* (Abstract of dissertation, Alliant International University, 2001), p. 17.

[16] P. Flowers and R. Shaw, 'Expanding the Evidence within Evidence-based Healthcare: Thinking about the Context, Acceptability and Feasibility of Interventions', paper presented to an IPA conference at Aston University, Birmingham, 2010.

2

CHILD SEXUAL ABUSE AND THE CATHOLIC CHURCH

N ONE OF THE priests I interviewed had themselves been the subject of child sex abuse allegations, or abuse allegations of any sort. But they were all part of the same Church structure and disciplines which were dealing with allegations and they were all aware of individual cases and how the Church was handling them. To varying degrees, all of them were aware that child sex abuse by some in the clergy has been an issue for the Catholic Church throughout its history. This was a common point of reference for my interviewees and for all priests.

Matthew and all of the five other priests I interviewed had been living in a society which received very extensive media coverage of child sex abuse allegations and their aftermath in England and Wales, coupled with extensive local coverage of the unfolding situations in Ireland, the United States and Australia where the vast majority of reported sexual abuse scandals in the Catholic Church had occurred. Together, all of these factors contributed to the milieu in which the priests lived and worked, and to the context in which their interviews with me took place.

Because of my previous role as a diocesan safeguarding coordinator I had more access to safeguarding matters on a national basis than did my interviewees. As an *ex-officio* member of the Anglophone Conference based at the Vatican, I had invaluable access to the unfolding story of the child abuse scandal at an international level. My position as a diocesan safeguarding co-ordinator for eleven years gave me the opportunity to attend more than thirty conferences both nationally and internationally and both Church and secular. Additionally, my academic studies in psychology at Boston College in the USA and at the University of Central Lancashire in Preston added greatly to the understanding of psychological processes and concepts, such as secondary victimhood and difficult conversations, which I and other priests receive during our formation. But as a serving parish priest, I shared the same point of reference and the same context as my interviewees and so I was aware how much this context had likely contributed to the views these priests would express in our interviews.

Priests in the structure of the Catholic Church

For those who are not familiar with it, the broad structure of the Catholic Church is provided for within the universal law of the Latin Church, the Code of Canon Law 1983. The following highly simplified summary captures some of the defining features of the relationships to which a priest becomes a party. Further, the provisions of Canon Law are themselves the expression of the Church's own theological understanding of priesthood and service.

The Church in England and Wales is divided into twenty-two dioceses, geographical areas which each come under the authority of a diocesan bishop. A religious order, whilst subject to the authority of a diocesan bishop, also has its own levels of accountability. A parish priest is answerable and accountable to his diocesan bishop; in a similar way, a priest from a religious order is accountable to his religious superior (head of the order). This account-ability does not detract from a priest's ultimate responsi-bility for the pastoral care of the people in his parish.

Authority is only exercised at various levels: world head (Pope), diocesan head (bishop, each of whom shares in hierarchical communion), local parish (priest). In the Eastern Churches, authority is also expressed at Patriarchal level. Currently, there are approximately 5,100 Catholic bishops around the world, each located in a cathedral that is the centre of administration, governance and control of the local churches (parishes) within its geographic territory.

Each parish has its own geographic territory and boundary lines. The parish priest is usually in charge of a single parish and has a responsibility for the Catholics living in it. In the Latin Catholic Church, only celibate men, as a rule, are ordained as priests. The Catholic Church and the ancient Christian churches see ordination as dedicating a person to a permanent relationship of service. The Canon Law Society of Great Britain and Ireland translates canon 519 of the Code of Canon Law to define the office of a parish priest:

> The parish priest is the proper pastor of the parish entrusted to him. He exercises the pastoral care of the community entrusted to him under the authority of the diocesan bishop, whose ministry of Christ he is called to share, so that for this community he may carry out the office of teaching, sanctifying and ruling with the co-operation of other priests or deacons and with the assistance of lay members of Christ's faithful, in accordance with the Law.

The priest answers only to his bishop and the Pope. A bishop from one diocese has no authority over a priest 'incardinated' (enlisted) within a different diocese. Priests are not employees or workers enjoying the protection of domestic labour laws. Unlike other denominations within the UK, the Catholic Church has not chosen to classify clergy in this way. But, following ordination, the ability to participate in the exercise of ministry by appointment to a particular office may be restricted or withdrawn. In terms of power and authority, only two men can 'fire' a priest: the Pope or the bishop of the diocese in which he is 'incardinated'. This dynamic is extremely relevant to the world view, or Gestalt, of all priests.

The concept of the brotherhood of the priesthood is significant for priests as the brotherhood far exceeds commonality and comradeship. When a man is ordained as a priest, the Church teaches that an ontological change takes place affecting nature and essence of being. The notion of ontological change and R. D. Laing's 1960 book *The Divided Self: An Existential Study in Sanity and Madness* bridge the gap between theology and psychology. I will explore these issues later.

The Catechism of the Catholic Church states that ordination 'confers an indelible spiritual character' which cannot be 'repeated or conferred temporarily' (c. 1582). C. 1583 further states that 'the vocation and mission received on the day of his ordination mark him permanently'. Ordination, like baptism and confirmation, is done once and for all. Holy Orders place one in a different position in the community, not a better or more privileged one, but a position from which one is called to spend a life exclusively in the service of the People of God.

Although writing about the Catholic Church in America, Franciscan theologian Fr Joseph Chinnici, OFM, provides an overall description of the Church and its priests which can be applied to the Church in England and Wales:

> As a social institution the Church claims moral authority: as a religious institution it claims truth and 'holiness'. Such has been its self-presentation in America since the early years of the immigrant Church, a public posture only strengthened during the era of the Cold War. As the Baltimore Catechism

> phrased it, 'Holy'—a central mark of the Church; it
> was a social body always teaching holy truths and
> making people holy. The public institutional carriers
> of that holiness were the priests and bishops who
> had received the sacraments of 'Holy Orders', and
> who administered the holy Sacraments.[1]

In accordance with the 1983 Code of Canon Law which governs the Latin Church, all parishioners (including children) have a right to receive spiritual help from their priest (canon 213). Canon 515 says the parish priest is tasked to prepare the faithful for the sacraments. This ought to come as no surprise. The office of parish priest is an ecclesiastical office. The priest is appointed to the office of parish priest to ensure the stability of ministry necessary for the good of the people entrusted to him.

The pastoral tasks and duties of the parish priest are outlined in canons 528 and 529 of the 1983 Code and include: 'to have a special care for the Catholic education of the young, to know the faithful entrusted to him through visits to families'. This raises the question of whether priests who no longer choose to engage in ministry with children and young people are failing to honour the demands of canon law. Many priests seem to have withdrawn from ministry and contact with children (based on my experience of conducting clergy safeguarding training).

An ancient problem for the Church

There is ample documentary evidence of the abuse of children by priests throughout almost two thousand years of Church history. One example serves to provide an insight into the history of the Church which the priests interviewed would have known to varying degrees from their formation.

Marcellin Champagnat, a young French priest in post-Napoleonic France, founded the Marist Brothers with the primary intention of teaching and providing religious education to poor children. When Champagnat came across abuse of children by members of the order, he acted swiftly to confront and discard offenders against children.[2]

In the early days of Champagnat's community, he took in children as boarders in order to boost funds. When he heard that one of his monks had yielded to 'temptation to impurity', Champagnat confronted the man with these words: 'What did that child do to you that you should rob him of his innocence? Away with you. You don't deserve mercy.'[3] In the context of his era in the early nineteenth century, he acted immediately and decisively.

For several years I attended the Anglophone Conference for Safeguarding at the Domus Sanctae Marthae, which is now the residence of Pope Francis. This is an international conference from the English-speaking Bishops' Conferences (countries). Opposite the front door to the main entrance is a statue of St Marcellin Champagnat. As someone who has been working in the field of safeguarding for more than twenty years, this statue epitomises for me what safeguarding should be about. The statue has St Marcellin comfortable in the presence of children and touching them appropriately. They are comfortable and safe in his presence, and are drawn to look to a larger horizon and a future full of hope. This captures the essence of ministry with children and young adults. It is in sharp contrast to a cartoon reproduced in *The Times* in April 2007 which depicted a priest leering at two altar boys from behind a gingerbread church. This cartoon epitomised not how priests viewed themselves, but how many priests believed people perceived them. Perhaps the most important challenge for priests today is how to reach the standards of pastoral ministry with children set by St Marcellin Champagnat.

In more recent times, individual cases caused sensational scandals in the 1970s, 1980s and 1990s. At that time, the bishops and religious superiors handled many individual cases either by moving the perpetrator to another assignment or sending him for treatment to one of the Church's own therapeutic facilities.[4] Thus, the first response of the Church was to handle any allegations or concerns 'in-house' without any reference to the civil statutory authorities. The very existence of specialised treatment centres shows that the Church was aware of this issue. The sad reality is that the sexual abuse of children has existed in all eras of Catholic Church history, and it is equally sad to see how the dynamics of abuse have not changed: the victims tend to be vulnerable children like orphans or those entrusted to the care of the Church.[5]

Child sex abuse in UK society

In the United Kingdom, cases involving the sexual abuse of children today are not confined to the Catholic Church. Since 1967, there have been at least thirty public or known private inquiries into abuse in children's homes and similar institutions, such as the public inquiry by Sir Cecil Clothier in 1994 and the Marcus Erooga inquiry in 2009 for the National Society for the Prevention of Cruelty to Children.

There has been a rise in public concern over sexual abuse generally within society and specifically across a range of institutions and professions. The media regularly carries news about the sexual abuse of minors by individuals and within institutions both religious and secular. The Rochdale Inquiry (2014), the Methodist Church (2015) inquiry, and the Doncaster and Oxford inquiries (2015) are just a few examples. The theme common to each of these enquiries is the systemic institutional aspect of the abuse of children.

The media have reported extensively on alleged abuses of children in the care of individuals and institutions, raising concern on the part not just of the general public but particularly of institutions which have looked into their own pasts. The media, for example, covered extensively a 2015 report for the Methodist Church in Britain entitled 'Courage, Cost and Hope' which found 102 allegations of sexual abuse by its ministers among nearly 2,000 cases of all forms of abuse by its clergy and lay people, some dating back to the 1950s.[6] Buckinghamshire Healthcare NHS Trust reported in February 2015 on 60 cases of sex abuse, many involving young children, by the late BBC personality Jimmy Saville at the Stoke Mandeville Hospital.

Even more public attention has been generated by high-profile allegations against Saville and other radio and television personalities, both living and dead, of sexually abusing children. In October 2012, the Metropolitan Police launched Operation Yewtree to investigate criminal charges in the Saville case. Some of these allegations, such as those against Saville and the BBC, have included investigations into decades of alleged institutional cover-ups that are reported, including by BBC News, to have concealed repeated abuses over many years.

The issue of child abuse is therefore a multidisciplinary matter, as are its implications for professionals who become secondary victims in all the affected fields. Claims and actual cases of abuse have impacted on the reputations of professionals and their continued confidence to work with children to such an extent that this issue has been discussed in the Children, Schools and Families Committee of the House of Commons. Unlike the priesthood, education is one area in which concern has been expressed for professionals innocent of any wrong-doing. In 2003, an Australian study into the impact of sexual abuse allegations against teachers found that the already very low percentage of male childcare staff dropped by half between 1992 and 1997 due in large part to allegations of sexual abuse against male teachers.[7]

In the UK, the National Union of Teachers reported in 2009 its concerns about rising levels of abuse allegations, although allegations against its members were mostly about physical restraint and discipline. In the same year, the National Association of Schoolmasters/Union of Women Teachers also suggested that there were signs that a culture of abuse allegations was spreading, a different type of secondary effect.

In UK legislation, the Children Act 1989 was the first major legislation on institutional abuse and provided measures to standardise practice in residential and day-care facilities. It provided a basis for the adoption of the 'paramountcy principle' which puts the protection of children first.

Legislation alone was clearly not sufficient as the government has continued to link legislation with the work done by non-governmental organisations, including faith communities. Following the 2003 murders of two girls by a school caretaker, the Bichard Inquiry (2004) led to the passage by Parliament of the Safeguarding Vulnerable Groups Act 2006 and the establishment of the Independent Safeguarding Authority (ISA). The ISA was established to co-ordinate professional and voluntary sectors to help prevent unsuitable people from working with children or vulnerable adults. It was merged with the Criminal Records Bureau in 2012 to form the Disclosure and Barring Service (DBS). Scotland has developed its own similar system, Disclosure Scotland, which works closely with the DBS. These services are mandated to keep potential abusers out of employment involving children and vulnerable adults; but their mandate does not extend to assisting innocent staff in employment areas where sexual abuse has nonetheless occurred. For example, the Manchester Safeguarding Children Board (MSCB) stated in 2007 that priority for children's security is a key principle.

Among other faith communities, the Church of England revisited policies and procedures in this arena in 'Protecting All God's Children'.[8] The Church of England, like the Catholic Church in England and Wales, also has published a policy to care for and supervise any member of the Church, ordained or lay, known to have offended against a child. The Churches' Child Protection Advisor Service (CCPAS), a Christian charity, is a resource for any Christian community seeking to either introduce or review safeguarding policies and procedures.

Among other recent major incidents in the United Kingdom, significant levels of child abuse have been recorded at a number of schools, hospitals, and care homes, and organised sexual abuse by sexual trafficking rings was revealed in Plymouth, Rotherham, Oxford, Rochdale, and Derby. An Independent Inquiry into Child Sexual Abuse was announced by then UK Home Secretary Rt Hon. Theresa May in July 2014 to examine how the country's institutions have handled their duty of care to protect children from sexual abuse.

Citing these cases and inquiries here illustrates the extent to which sexual abuse is all too evident in the United Kingdom. It is not meant to minimise the reality of Catholic clergy child sex abuse nor to suggest that priests' sexual misconduct is just the overflow of a societal problem. Rather, these cases provide continuing reminders of this most scandalous occurrence to non-offending priests such as those I interviewed and to the communities in which they live.

Media coverage of the global situation in the Catholic Church

Other reminders for non-offending priests in England and Wales and for their communities have also come from the scandals in other countries which have been widely publicised in the UK. The priests I would interview were familiar with these international cases, especially those in Ireland where two extensive published reports were released in 2009 (the Ryan Report and the Murphy Report) on child sex abuse in the Catholic Church. There have also been media reports of abuse by priests in England, Wales and Scotland and revelations of abuse have emerged in Germany, the Netherlands, and Belgium.

In Australia in 2010, Archbishop Mark Coleridge, then Archbishop of Canberra and Goulburn and now Archbishop of Brisbane and a member of the Pontifical Council for Social Communications, wrote in a letter for Pentecost on the crisis and its effects. In the letter, entitled 'Seeing the faces, hearing the voices', he wrote: 'The story of the sexual abuse of the young within the Catholic Church has been the greatest drama of my thirty-six years of priesthood.'[9]

An Australian Royal Commission into Institutional Responses to Child Sexual Abuse was appointed in November 2012 to investigate how the Catholic Church, other churches and other institutions in Australia dealt with allegations and incidents of child sex abuse. Nearly five years later, it is still investigating thousands of allegations against many institutions and the Catholic Church's alleged covering up of allegations has been at the centre of its inquiries.

In the United States, one of the other countries with much published material on the subject, media revelations of clergy sexual abuse of minors began to surface as early as 1990. A dramatic change took place after the 'Boston Crisis' of 2002 which was the first time the scale of abuse of children by clergy was widely reported in a public arena.

Allegations by victims, reporters and litigators forced the US to confront what one 2011 report in the country's Catholic newspaper the *National Catholic Reporter* described as an internal cancer. Among the responses was the self-examination of its priests' attitudes by Msgr Rossetti which found that priests reported they were happy in their work.

In June 2002, a Charter for the Protection of Children and Young People was approved by the United States Conference of Catholic Bishops. It created a National Review Board which was instructed to commission a study, with the co-operation of the dioceses and eparchies, of the nature and scope of sexual abuse of minors by clergy. The board engaged the John Jay College of Criminal Justice of the City University of New York to analyse allegations of sexual abuse in dioceses in the United States from 1950 to 2002. The result was a report titled 'The Causes and Context of Sexual Abuse of Minors by Catholic Priests in the United States', commonly known as the John Jay Report (2010).

The report found 10,667 people had alleged sexual abuse. Of these, the dioceses identified 6,700 unique accusations against 4,392 clergy, which was about four per cent of the 109,694 ordained priests, deacons, or members of religious orders active in the US. Of the 4,392 accused, 252 (5.7 per cent of those accused or less than 0.1 per cent of total clergy) were convicted. The number of alleged abuses increased in the 1960s and 1970s, then declined in the 1980s and by the next decade had fallen to 1950s levels. Fifteen years before the John Jay Report, other studies had estimated a slightly high percentage of offending priests, putting the figure at six per cent, with eighty per cent of those offending against adolescent boys while the remainder targeted younger children. These studies also expressed the view that this crisis was not confined to the Catholic Church and that incidents of such abuse are also perpetrated by Protestant, Jewish, and other religious groups.

While the Church has experienced such cases historically, the intense global media attention directed at these cases in recent years is new and relentless, with the result that the public are given the impression that many priests are sex offenders and that the problem is a recent one, factors that contribute to the concept of non-offending priests as secondary victims. The unfortunate alliteration of 'paedophile' and 'priest' does nothing to help this inaccurate impression.[10] As Brid Fahey Bates has noted in her history of the Rosminian Order, the Institute of Charity which has served Ireland for more than a century and a half mainly with schools for boys, it seems that the Catholic Church has received the most attention for its offenders.[11]

In 2010, German journalist and author Peter Seewald, in noting that priests reportedly formed 0.03 per cent of people convicted of child abuse in the United States, put this point to Pope Benedict XVI in a very direct question: 'Is the Catholic Church being watched differently and evaluated differently with regard to abuse?' To which the Pope replied:

> If you look at the real statistics, that does not authorise us to look away from the problem or to minimise it. But we must also note that in these

matters we are not dealing with something specific to the Catholic priesthood or the Catholic Church.[12]

The Church's handling of the scandals

My remarks, which some bishops found offensive, were deadly accurate. I make no apology. To resist grand jury subpoenas, to suppress the names of offending clerics, to deny, to obfuscate, to explain away; that is the model of a criminal organization [*sic*], not my Church.[13]

Victims have never been treated in a compassionate way, given the damage that has been done to them. Church leaders have known about this kind of behaviour throughout the Church's history. Church leaders have abused their power to protect clergy offenders and stop the crimes being made public. The penalties imposed have generally been lenient, and the Church often only acted when it had to.[14]

The first description above of the Church's initial response to clergy child sex abuse allegations came from Frank Keating, a former Governor of Oklahoma in the United States and a former Federal Bureau of Investigation officer, whose forthright views caused him to resign as chair of the American Church's National Review Board. The second description sums up many similar opinions of the Church's handling of the scandals found in official reports, the media and academic publications. My interviews sought to gauge whether the Church's handling of the scandals had affected the six priests in my sample. Their reactions to the policies of denial and cover-up that the Church initially pursued and the role of bishops in the implementation of those policies came through clearly in our discussions, as their own comments and my analysis reveal.

Colm O'Gorman, a victim of clerical sexual abuse, described his experience of the response he received from the institutional Church thus:

> When I turned to the Church that purported to be the Church of the living Christ, I was met not with love and truth, but with lies and obfuscation. The denial and deceit of the hierarchy of the institutional Catholic Church was a final and terrible revelation of the corruption of its values.[15]

In Ireland, Bishop Jim Moriarty of the Diocese of Kildare and Leighlin, who resigned after the publication of the Murphy Report in 2009, wrote to the people of his diocese: 'I fully accept that the attempts by Church authorities to "protect the Church" and "avoid scandal" had the most dreadful consequences for children and were deeply wrong.' He added:

> Nor does it serve the truth to overlook the fact that the system of management and communications within the archdiocese [of Dublin] was seriously flawed. However, with the benefit of hindsight, I accept that, from the time I became an auxiliary bishop, I should have challenged the prevailing culture.[16]

Speaking at a canon law conference that I attended in Washington, DC, in July 2004, Rev. John P. Beal, JCD, of the School of Canon Law at the Catholic University of America, spoke of the overwhelming evidence that bishops throughout the world sought to protect the Church's image by denying or minimising complaints. Moreover, where there was acknowledgment, it expressed itself with the primary concern for the reputation of the abusing priest rather that his victims or for the prevention of further abuse. Many bishops were reportedly so consumed by the need to protect the reputation of the Church that they were, as Rev. Beal put it, 'paralysed by the cancer eating away at the heart of the Catholic Church'.

Canon law and a new direction

The Church's handling of the abuse scandal raises difficult questions about the relative order of civil, criminal and canon law in society. It also raised questions about whether canon law was applied properly, as the report of Ireland's Murphy Commission of Investigation noted:

> Canon law provides the Church authorities with a means not only of dealing with offending clergy, but also with a means of doing justice to victims, including paying compensation to them. In practice, it appears to the Commission that, for a significant part of the period covered by the Commission, canon law was used selectively when dealing with offending clergy, to the benefit of the cleric and the consequent disadvantage of his victims. The commission has not encountered a case where canon law was invoked as a means of doing justice to victims.[17]

Questions were also raised about whether canon law was applied properly in cases where non-offending priests were wrongly accused:

> The niceties of canon law, due process and elementary decency have in many instances taken a beating. As one cardinal archbishop said ... it may be necessary for some priests to suffer injustice for the good of the Church. In the course of history, Caiaphas has not been without his defenders ... Another reaction claims to be realistic, which is to say hard-nosed: it is too bad that some innocent priests may be hurt, but you cannot make an omelette without breaking eggs, etc. Charming.

But then, bishops have their own leadership credibility to worry about.[18]

This position is in direct contradiction of the Church's
Code of Canon Law and the advice given by the Roman
Curia, the Church's administrative structure based in
Rome, about safeguarding.

In his extensive 2010 papal interview with Peter Seewald, Pope Benedict XVI regarded the sexual abuse of
children by priests as 'so much filth'. The Pope described
it as almost like 'the crater of a volcano'.[19] Writing in *The
Furrow* in 2002, University College Dublin researcher Dr
Marie Keenan noted: 'Above all, the priesthood suddenly
seemed to be a place of shame and every priest was under
the suspicion of being one like that too.'

Dr Keenan further reports that, at least for the clergy
in Ireland, the crisis produced unforeseen consequences,
creating significant problems. In Ireland, new groups of
secondary casualties were emerging, primarily priests who
were seemingly falsely accused. Priests on both sides of
the Irish Sea perceived that priests who were falsely
accused were regarded as 'collateral damage'.[20] Other
research I have conducted amongst priests in England and
Wales confirmed Keenan's research. 'False' allegations
were a great concern of the priests attending the training
sessions I have been involved with as the great majority of
priests in England and Wales are innocent. I tested this
with my new interviews.

It can be argued that the Church's current treatment
of accused priests, whether innocent or guilty, still ignores
its own canon law as Canon number 384 provides:

With special solicitude, a diocesan bishop is to
attend to presbyters and listen to them as assistants
and counsellors. He is to protect their rights and
take care they fulfil the obligations proper to their

> state and that the means and institutions which
> they need to foster spiritual and intellectual life are
> available to them.
>
> He is also to take care that provision is made for
> their decent support and social assistance accord-
> ing to the norms of law.

However, serious criticisms from a legal perspective were aimed at the Church's failure to report accusations to the police. In response, some American legislators, such as those in 2002 in Massachusetts, changed the law to make reporting of abuse to police compulsory for the clergy of all religious denominations. *An Act Requiring Certain Religious Officials to Report Abuse of Children* spells out what the Catholic Church and all religious bodies in Massachusetts must do in the event of an accusation against a priest.

The Church began addressing most of its failings in the abuse crisis globally, including some reforms which were completed before my interviews and of which the six priests should have been aware.

The Vatican, which is an independent principality, in 1990 was amongst the first countries to ratify the 1989 United Nations Convention of the Rights of the Child. But it was to take another two decades, two inquiries in Britain (Nolan, 2001, and Cumberlege, 2007), two in Ireland (Ryan and Murphy in 2009), and one in the United States (John Jay, 2011) before the Church implemented the UN convention in its handling of its child sex abuse cases.

The UN Committee on the Convention of the Rights of the Child met in January 2014 in Geneva and the Vatican appeared before it to report on its implementation of the convention. The Vatican was described in a 20 July editorial in *The Tablet* as taking a first step towards restoring its good name over clerical child sexual abuse.

The editorial noted that its record was not impressive as no bishop had been dismissed for negligent handling of clergy responsible for the sexual abuse of children. This is in sharp contrast to the response of Pope Francis who reportedly said at his morning mass on 16 January that some cases have cost the Church a lot of money. *L'Osservatore Romano*, the semi-official daily newspaper of the Vatican, quoted the Pope as exclaiming: 'Good! One must do that … the shame of the Church!'

The Tablet editorial on 20 January went on to ask why the Vatican had not told all bishops that failure to comply with the strict letter and spirit of the UN convention, which gives absolute priority to the child's interest, would be grounds for dismissal? Bishop Charles Scicluna, who is also the Vatican's former chief prosecutor of child sex abuse cases, reportedly informed the UN committee that Pope Benedict had laicised 384 priest abusers between 2011 and 2012 and voluntarily and forcibly removed another 182. The editorial insisted this would be normal in any civilised secular society. Having ratified the convention, the Vatican was expected to be judged by those standards if not higher, given the Church's stand on ethical and moral issues.

Pope Francis established the Pontifical Commission for the Protection of Minors on 5 December 2013 and subsequently appointed its members, including lay people and women from five continents. The first task of the commission—to draft statutes defining its competence and role—was completed and published on 8 May 2015. The Director of the Holy See Press Office, Fr Federico Lombardi, SJ, said that the commission would contribute to 'the safety of young people'. He also stressed in *L'Osservatore Romano* on 22 March 2014 that in establishing the commission Pope Francis was 'continuing the commitment undertaken by his predecessors, and having heard the advice of a number of cardinals, other members of the College of Bishops and experts in the field'. So far, the Pontifical Commission has not been empowered to address the problems of non-offending priests nor to consider them as possible secondary victims.

Bishop Scicluna, speaking for the Congregation for the Doctrine of the Faith in the Vatican, said in 2013 that the Church should be committed, in fairness and justice, to humbly acknowledging the problem with total and unequivocal respect for the truth.

In the Church in England and Wales, Lord Nolan was commissioned in 2000 to review its child protection. His review, completed in 2001, led to the establishment of the Catholic Office for the Protection of Children and Vulnerable Adults (COPCA). Nolan also recommended a further review after five years. The Cumberlege Commission carried out that review and in its 2007 report 'Safeguarding with Confidence' recommended new national safeguarding structures which the Church adopted from 1 July 2008, well before my interviews.

Cumberlege started from the principle that safeguarding is an integral part of the mission of the Catholic Church: 'Being loved and being kept safe go to the very core of the Church's ministry to children and vulnerable adults.' It recommended that the term 'safeguarding' be used instead of 'protection' to emphasise that this is proactive work to prevent abuse taking place, not simply reacting and responding to allegations, although this remains a key part of the work. The commission very strongly supported the aim of a 'one Church' approach, with the dioceses and religious congregations jointly owning the work and the safeguarding structures.

This current approach is in keeping with the Church's ancient traditions. St Benedict, the Patron Saint of Europe and the founder of the Benedictine order of religious monks, proclaimed that the Church is at its strongest when it works on the margins. The literature on the Catholic Church, with approximately 220,000 parishes in the Church worldwide, rates it as the world's second largest international development body after the United Nations. More than half of African hospitals are operated by faith-based organisations, with the Catholic Church in Africa providing nearly one quarter of all healthcare. Globally, the Catholic Church is one of the biggest healthcare providers. As of April 2014, it runs 5,246 hospitals, 17,530 dispensaries, 577 leprosy clinics, and 15,208 houses for the elderly, chronically ill, and people with physical and learning disabilities. A quarter of all Africa's HIV care comes from Catholic Church agencies. The Church provides approximately 12 million school places a year in sub-Saharan Africa, offering education to help many millions of young Africans to escape from poverty.[21]

These examples clearly indicate the Church's commitment to those on the margins of society and provide the context against which clerical sexual abuse of minors has taken place. But this commitment fails to explain why safeguarding the marginalised victims of sexual abuse has not been given the same status as its care for other marginalised sections within society even though the 'paramountcy principle' from the 1989 Children Act was adopted by the Bishops' Conference of England and Wales in 2001 to put the rights of children first. Nor does it explain how the Church could fail to see how others are also affected by these crises.

Catholic social teaching is the body of Church doctrine covering matters of social justice. Although its origins can be traced to the writings of St Augustine of Hippo (354–430) and St Thomas Aquinas (1255–1274), it is also derived from concepts present in the Old and New Testaments. According to Pope Benedict XVI in his first Encyclical dated 25 December 2005, the purpose of Catholic social teaching

> is simply to purify reason and contribute, here and now, to the acknowledgement and attainment of what is just ... [The Church] has to play her part through rational argument and she has to reawaken spiritual energy without which justice ... cannot prevail and prosper.[22]

Integral to Catholic social teaching is the 'preferential option for the poor'. This refers to a trend throughout the Judeo-Christian scriptures of giving preference to the well-being of the poor and powerless. Accordingly, this doctrine implies that the moral test of any society is

> how it treats its most vulnerable members. The poor have the most urgent moral claim on the conscience of the nation. We are called to look at public policy decisions in terms of how they affect the poor.[23]

In a 7 July 2014 address given at *Domus Sanctae Marthae*, the Pope's Residence, to victims of clerical sexual abuse, Pope Francis unequivocally stated his support for victims when he declared in a Homily:

> This is what causes me distress and pain at the fact that some priests and bishops, by sexually abusing minors, violated their innocence and their own priestly vocation. It is something more than despicable actions. It is like a sacrilegious cult, because these boys and girls had been entrusted to the priestly charism in order to be brought to God. And those people sacrificed them to the idol of

their own concupiscence … Before God and his people, I express my sorrow for the sins and grave crimes of clerical sexual abuse committed against you. And I humbly ask forgiveness.

This papal statement is the most precise statement by the Church leadership on this issue. It came decades after the crisis started to emerge, and two years after my interviews.

Notes

1   J. Chinnici, *When Values Collide* (Berkeley, CA, USA: Orbis Books, 2010), p. 157.
2   B. Geary and J. M. Greer (eds), *The Dark Night of the Catholic Church* (Stowmarket, SFK, UK: Kevin Mayhew, 2011), pp. 39–42.
3   J.-B. Furet, *The Life of Joseph-Benoît Marcellin Champagnat, 1789-1840* (Rome: Marist Brothers, 1856), p. 409.
4   Geary and Greer (eds), *The Dark Night of the Catholic Church*.
5   *Ibid.*
6   Methodist Church Past Cases Review, *Courage, Cost and Hope* (London: Methodist Church, 2015), available at: http://www.methodist.org.uk/media/1683823/past-cases-review-2013-2015-final.pdf.
7   L. Mellor and J. Sachs, 'Child panic and child protection policy: A critical examination of policies from New South Wales and Queensland', a paper presented to the *Educational Research, Risks and Dilemmas Joint Conference of the Australian and New Zealand Associations for Research in Education Annual Conference*, Auckland, New Zealand, 2003.
8   Church of England, *Protecting & Safeguarding Children and Adults* (London: Church of England, 2015), available at: https://www.churchofengland.org/clergy-office-holders/protecting-and-safeguarding-children-and-adults-who-are-vulnerable.aspx.
9   M. B. Coleridge, *Seeing the Faces, Hearing the Voices* (Catholic Diocese of Wollongong, 2010), *available at:* http://www.dow.org.au/news/news-and-media/item/seeing-the-faces-hearing-the-voices?category_id=4.
10 T. G. Plante, 'Introduction: What do we know about Roman Catholic priests who sexually abuse minors?' in *Bless Me Father*

for I Have Sinned: Perspectives on Sexual Abuse Committed by Roman Catholic Priests (Westport, CT, USA: Praeger, 1999), pp. 1–6.

[11] B. Fahey Bates, *The Institute of Charity: Rosminians, Their Irish Storey 1860–2003* (Dublin: Ashfield Press, 2003).

[12] P. Seewald, *Benedict XVI: An Intimate Portrait* (San Francisco: Ignatius Press, 2008), p. 92.

[13] Geary and Greer (eds), *The Dark Night of the Catholic Church*, p. 91.

[14] T. P. Doyle, et al., *Sex, Priests and Secret Codes: The Catholic Church's 2,000-Year Paper Trail of Sexual Abuse* (Los Angeles: Volt Press, 2005), p. 63.

[15] Geary and Greer (eds), *The Dark Night of the Catholic Church*, p. 71.

[16] *Ibid.*, p. 101.

[17] Murphy Commission of Investigation, *Report into the Catholic Archdiocese of Dublin* (Dublin: Department of Justice and Equality, Government of Ireland, 2009), pp. 57–58.

[18] R. J. Neuhaus, 'In the aftermath of scandal', *First Things* February/2004, pp. 58–76.

[19] Seewald, *Benedict XVI: An Intimate Portrait*, p. 23.

[20] M. Keenan, *Child Sexual Abuse and the Catholic Church: Gender, Power, and Organizational Culture* (New York: Oxford University Press, 2011), p. 224.

[21] F. Campbell, 'The Catholic Church and the British government' in *Magnificat—Liturgies and Events of the Papal Visit of Pope Benedict XVI to the United Kingdom* (London: Catholic Communications Network, 2010).

[22] Pope Benedict XVI, *Deus caritas est,* 28(a).

[23] G. Gutierrez, *A Theology of Liberation: History, Politics and Salvation* (Maryknoll, NY, USA: Orbis Books, 1973), p. 68.

3

Six Ground-Breaking Discussions

OVER A PERIOD of several months starting in 2012, I conducted separate interviews with Matthew and each of the other five selected priests. Matthew and four of his brother priests belonged to a diocese overseen by a bishop, while the sixth priest was from a religious order overseen by a religious superior. The six proved to be a varied group of priests as regards number of years ordained and where they exercised their ministry within England and Wales. Whilst they were bound by all being Catholic priests working in England and Wales, they each presented in a unique way during their interview. The number of years ordained and the places they worked were idiosyncratic for each of the interviewees. All six provided very rich data and contributed uniquely to the content of this study.

Because I examined their human existence in detail, opening up subjective experiences concerning extremely delicate and sensitive issues in their lives, I refer to them here by pseudonyms—Matthew, Philip, Anthony, Daniel, Christopher, and Gerald—to preserve their privacy. I then undertook a line-by-line analysis of the transcribed text of each interview, identifying emergent themes within and across the interviews. I organised all the data into a format that allowed analysis to be traced right through the process.

I then reflected on my own perceptions, conceptions, and processes. As this involved extraordinary and sensitive moral and ethical issues, I found it necessary to access increased supervision from my second university supervisor, Dr Liz Ballinger. I was concerned that the findings did not contain any 'good news'. Having acknowledged that, my supervisor went on to enquire as to the current whereabouts of the priests whom I interviewed. I informed her that each of my interviewees was a non-offending priest and that each of them was still in post and content. She remarked that, given the overarching superordinate themes, this was very surprising. It was this comment that sparked a 'eureka' moment which made me realise that, perhaps due to the fact that I am an insider researcher, I initially missed significant themes which I then realised were in plain sight. The superordinate themes below therefore do reveal some surprising 'good news'. As St Paul wrote to the Christians in Corinth in 57 AD:

> We are in difficulties on all sides, but never cornered; we see no answer to our problems, but never despair; we have been persecuted, but never deserted; knocked down, but never killed; always, wherever we may be, we carry with us the suffering of Christ. (2 Co 4:8–11)

Each interviewee was aware that I was both a researcher and a fellow priest who had previously been a diocesan safeguarding co-ordinator and had been responsible for interviewing some of the priests accused of sexual abuse against children. My position as a brother priest seemed to far outweigh the role of a safeguarding co-ordinator. As will be seen, all of the priests were willing to share extensively their views of their experiences as priests in ministry during this crisis. Each interviewee spoke freely and candidly from the moment our conversation began until the recorder was switched off at the end of the interview. I did not feel I had to build a 'therapeutic alliance' to enable the priests to share their personal experiences with me. This greatly assisted our discussions and my dual role of priest and researcher, far from being a problem, appeared to facilitate my research. The level of trust that I experienced with each participant permitted me to be confident that my findings were genuine and the results worth analysing.

During the semi-structured interviews, the first question asked of each of the participants pertained to their journey to the priesthood. The purposes of this introductory question were: to ease the way into a conversation, which in turn would facilitate a deeper encounter; to gain some appreciation of the participants' unique journey to priesthood and their unique experience of being a priest; and to enable me to compare and contrast participants' perceptions in the light of what most of them described as the 'explosion' of the Church's child abuse scandal. The journey to priesthood for each of the participants seemed to have a unique and profound effect on their perception of the 'brotherhood of priests' and to affect their perception of the Church as an establishment and their role within it.

Whilst the focus of the study was an exploration of the effect on priests working in England and Wales, each of the candidates referred to the scandal in other parts of the world, especially the Church in North America, Ireland and Australia. The Boston child abuse crisis of 2002 and reports that were published in Ireland in 2009 (the Ryan Report and the Murphy Report) were referred to by all interviewees. Each interviewee viewed the universal Roman Catholic Church as 'one body' so anything that happened anywhere in the Church affected the whole Church. Each interviewee referred to the sexual abuse of children by priests in other parts of the world and reported that the crisis outside England and Wales had a profoundly detrimental effect on him. Unknowingly, each repeated Dr Joanne Greer's principal symptom of secondary victimhood almost word for word.

The interviews produced near unanimity. As the following table shows, their comments on the effects of the scandal on them can be divided into eight broad overarching superordinate themes and then subdivided into subordinate themes.[1] All six commented on seven of the themes and five commented on the remaining theme. It should be noted from the outset that these superordinate themes were not necessarily chronological and on many occasions overlapped each other.

Table 3.1 Findings by themes

Superordinate themes	Number of interviewees raising this theme	Subordinate themes
An Existential Crisis	5	• Holocaust • Earth-shattering/horrific • Unbelievable • Feeling of being overwhelmed
Grief and Loss	6	• Loss of core identity • Loss of authority and lack of confidence in the institutional Church • Loss of reference point
Fear	6	• Fear for the future of the Church • Fear of false allegations • Fear of working with children

Superordinate themes	Number of interviewees raising this theme	Subordinate themes
Betrayal	6	• Betrayal by perpetrators • Betrayal by Church authorities (national and international)
Shame and Isolation	6	• Collectively branded • Adverse media coverage • Ridicule and humiliation • Stigma
Impasse	6	• Tension between reconciling clergy perpetrators and justice for victims • Lack of leadership from bishops
Lack of Confidence in the Institutional Church as regards this issue	6	• Lack of openness and transparency • Disillusionment
Resilience and Commitment	6	• Loyalty • Tenacity • Forgiveness • Faith

Superordinate theme 1: Existential crisis

The interviewees reported that their experience of the child abuse scandal was, in the words of one of them, a 'tectonic' shift, which implies overtones of something fundamental, foundational. Apart from one who was recently ordained,

the interviewees described how both the scandal and the
initial mishandling by Church authorities had a profoundly
negative effect on their identity as priests and their opinion
of those Church authorities. By mishandling I am referring
to their accounts of bishops initially refusing to believe
what was going on, and then seeking to protect the institutional reputation of the Church at all costs. This alleged
mishandling was, according to my interviewees, compounded by the bishops' seemingly 'hanging out to dry'
anyone against whom an allegation was made. Over half
the interviewees used this phrase to describe their fear of
being abandoned by their bishop/religious superior if an
allegation was made against them.

Their reaction can be accurately described as a crisis—a
moment of judgement—because it affected the very core
of who they were aspiring to be. Thus it was a crisis which
can accurately be described as existential in nature. In
particular, the crisis lies in the fact that they reported
fundamental changes in how they viewed other priests and
how they perceived themselves to be viewed by lay Catholics within the Church. The issue seriously dented their
confidence as priests both in themselves and in the
establishment they served. These points are further
detailed in the following subordinate themes.

Holocaust

One of the main themes to arise from the interviews was
the complete sense of horror and disbelief as the scandal
unfolded. One of my interviewees chose to describe this
by using the word 'holocaust', a word that has strong
emotive connotations. The use of the word indicates the
profound effect that this experience had on the lives and
perceptions of these priests and helps the reader to get in

touch with the stark reality of how difficult this experience has been for them.

> There is no denying ... this is almost like a holocaust. (Matthew)

> I can't believe this. No one could make it up. (Philip)

Despite being aware of the emotive connotations associated with the word holocaust, as the researcher I felt obliged to report my interviewees' experience and views as accurately as I could. Whilst I was not surprised to learn that my interviewees were shocked by the child abuse scandal, I was taken aback by the profound effect it had on their identity as priests. I was aware, anecdotally, that priests were having a difficult time coming to terms with the crisis; but my research brought me in touch with the stark reality of just how difficult some priests have found the crisis, and the effects, both long- and short-term, it has had on them.

Earthshattering/horrific

> This is the worst thing that has ever happened to me as a priest. (Matthew)

> Being exposed to the scandal has defiled my innocence. (Matthew)

> The first disclosure I heard changed me forever. (Philip)

These quotes are further evidence that the priests I interviewed felt shattered by the abuse crisis. The quotes are very explicit and unambiguously report a very significant, almost traumatic, experience. The interviewees said that the crisis was the worst thing that ever happened to them as their innocence was defiled and their lives were changed forever, hence the existential nature of their reaction.

> I was thrown straight into the horror of it. It caused
> tectonic changes. (Philip)

> Well … I was horrified. He was a priest and part of
> a paedophile ring. (Daniel)

These quotes proved further evidence of the overwhelming impact this crisis had on the day-to-day ministry of the interviewees. Reports of 'tectonic changes' and horror cannot be taken lightly. The language used by the interviewees and the level of hurt and distress the crisis caused them indicates the possibility of psychological distress.

Unbelievable

> It was the shock. It was especially pronounced
> because it was against children, my predecessor
> here was imprisoned. (Christopher)

This particular quote refers to the first time that one of my interviewees disclosed that he had been appointed to replace a priest who was a convicted child abuser. It raises the first account of split loyalties between the offending brother priest and the victim. For this priest, the split loyalties were further complicated by the fact that the parishioners in the parish he had inherited were themselves victims of split loyalties. Some parishioners simply refused to believe that their previous parish priest was guilty; others believed that, even if he was guilty, he should be forgiven.

This conflict will be familiar to diocesan safeguarding co-ordinators who have to go to a parish to address the issue of the removal or arrest of a parish priest and its impact on the parishioners. In my own experience, I remember some parishioners making the unfortunate comment that 'it takes two to tango', a comment also made by some of the interviewees. Priests who are asked to succeed a predecessor who has been removed, arrested, or convicted of child abuse are, more often than not, asked to do so without any input or guidance as to how to support parishioners as they process the news in their different ways. This was echoed in the responses from one of the priests I interviewed.

> My initial reaction was denial, really. I thought it must be some sort of anti-clericalism. Then more and more cases came out of Ireland, and then all the problems in America. (Daniel)

The depth of betrayal felt by the interviewees was very pronounced. Their first reaction was to assume it was either untrue or exaggerated. This was a position, as will be seen below, they quickly moved away from. Interviewees who expressed this view went on to explain that when the crisis initially erupted there was little or no communication between bishops and their priests. This meant that the interviewees not only had to respond to and process the crisis personally, but they also felt that they were left in the dark by the bishops as to what they could and could not say. The shock of what happened, which they described as 'unbelievable', was not initially addressed. The interviewees reported an experience of floundering which was compounded by their experience of being kept in the dark.

Feeling of being overwhelmed

> I feel absolutely drained by this. (Matthew)

> I don't understand what goes on with a paedophile. I don't want to know. It's exhausting just coping with all this stuff. I feel contaminated. (Philip)

All of the interviewees expressed concern about the fact that, as regards being able to comprehend the reasons for the scandal, along with trying to rationalise the bishops' initial response, they felt both unprepared and out of their depth. This experience resonated with similar experiences of being left to flounder and grapple with something that was far beyond their comfort zone. They expressed a feeling of being exposed by a system they trusted. Five of the six interviewees expressed concern about and a lack of confidence in the way that the Church had prepared them during their seminary formation.

They inadvertently displayed symptoms of grief for the loss of a Church they thought they knew. Some voiced fear for their future ministry and fear for the future of the Church. This is a theme which is developed in greater detail in the superordinate theme of resilience and commitment below. This does not negate the fact that the fears reported at the time were genuine and were accompanied with the understandable anxiety they generated. Some of the interviewees reported an inability to know who to trust, something that they had never experienced in their priesthood. They felt misled and betrayed, and that it occasionally led them to feelings of despair. These descriptions generated in me, as the researcher, an increasing concern for the long-term psychological welfare of these men. They went on to report an increasing sense of injustice and anxiety about themselves as possible collateral damage. By this they meant anxiety about being deserted by their bishop if an accusation of child abuse was made about them. This particular anxiety had a profoundly detrimental effect on their relationship with their own bishop and their view of the institutional Church.

Five of the six interviewees reported a loss of confidence in the Church authorities, whom they considered to be more interested in the good name of the institution rather than the welfare of victims and innocent priests. Interestingly, the only priest who did not share this view was the priest who had only been ordained for two years. This particular priest was unique among the interviewees because he was the only priest to be trained and ordained after the abuse scandal had been exposed. This theme, in many ways, encapsulates other themes as differing responses of fear, a sense of betrayal, loss and others came together in the form of a personal existential crisis for these priests.

Superordinate theme 2: Grief and loss

Grief and loss were articulated by these men on several levels. In the first instance, they reported a loss of confidence in Church authorities whom they previously trusted. Secondly, they said they felt a sense of loss in respect of their own identity and in relation to their role in the Church more generally. The interviewees all reported that the scandal had caused them for the first time to feel that the general public had doubts about trusting them. Last but not least, their sense of grief and loss also related to a sense of being betrayed by brother priests, which was accompanied by uncertainty about who, amongst their brother priests, could be trusted. This experience, perhaps more than any, profoundly impacted on the later superordinate theme of betrayal, which is explored in more detail below.

Loss of identity

> There is immaturity in us about lots of things. As a priest, a big eye-opener was realising I had a very puerile relationship with my bishop. That's not unusual: priest to bishop, priest to people, we need to grow up. (Philip)

This particular quote is significant because it was said by a priest who had been ordained for many years. It was the first time that the notion of institutional dysfunctionality had been introduced. The quote infers that if the Church was not so dysfunctional as an organisation, then this crisis might not have happened, or it would at least have been handled more justly. This has relevance to a sense of loss of identity and focus because, perhaps for the first time, this priest was beginning to have serious reservations about the integrity of the organisational structure of which he was a part. This particular interviewee went on to extrapolate what he regarded as other symptoms of dysfunctionality, such as in the way the institution handles its financial affairs. It is interesting to hear a very experienced priest suggest that the child abuse scandal seemed to have, somewhat inadvertently, lifted the lid on institutionalised dysfunctionality. This loss of identity and focus is understandable given the particular relationship that exists between a bishop and his priests, which will be discussed at greater length in chapter five.

> A number of priests think that their bishop should be defending them. It was very painful trying to have good, open relationships between priests and bishops. There is little support for priests and a lot of ignorance on the part of priests. They are ignorant of procedures and ignorant of protection for anyone else. (Philip)

> I still have a feeling that if it meant hanging one of us out to dry, he [the bishop] would. I don't know if that would be for the sake of the children or the Church. (Gerald)

These quotes refer to an undermining of the whole point of reference for the interviewees. It raises the very concerning prospect that these priests feel that their very identity and their place in the Church have been taken from them. This injustice is compounded by their innocence as regards the child abuse crisis. Five of the six interviewees expressed concern about brother priests whom they either knew personally or had heard about and who they felt had been treated unjustly in response to an allegation of child abuse. Most of the interviewees felt that if a malicious allegation should be made against one of their brother priests, the bishop would 'hang them out to dry'. The truth or otherwise of these stories did not detract from the fact that they feared that in similar circumstances this could also happen to them. This left them with a feeling of being exposed, which in turn fostered their feeling of loss of identity and focus. These views are expanded upon in even more detail below.

Loss of authority and lack of confidence in the institutional Church

> Cover-up by Church authorities is worst because it's systemic. (Matthew)

> The biggest shock was that the Church was more concerned with its image than with doing the right thing. (Gerald)

> It made me question the Church. Why didn't the bishops realise? (Daniel)

Whilst each interviewee reported a sense of shock at the child abuse scandal, their experience of the institutional Church's initial response had a very damaging effect on their attitude towards the bishops of England and Wales. All of the interviewees reported that, in their view, the child abuse crisis caused two scandals. The first scandal was the fact that the abuses took place at all, and the second was that the bishops of England and Wales seemed to respond so ineffectually. All of the interviewees reported that the second scandal was harder to bear and had a more negatively profound effect on them than the fact that brother priests were guilty of such atrocious acts.

Loss of reference point leading to a lack of trust

> The Church has lost its moral high ground. People are saying, 'We can't trust them, they are all paedophiles'. (Daniel)

> There's a lack of confidence about lack of professionalism in the Church. (Philip)

> Their solution is to get priests to say more prayers and to separate them [from lay students studying theology] during formation. It's so naïve; it's not grappling with the issues. (Gerald)

The relationship between a priest and his bishop is different from the relationship between an employer and an employee. In the Church, this relationship is based on trust. On ordination, a priest enters into a life-long 'covenant' which includes as a central component a mutual commitment to the Church's teaching and to the bishop and his successors. This two-way relationship is stipulated in canon 384 of the 1983 Code of Canon Law, under which the bishop must secure the welfare of his priests and actively promote it. It would seem that, at least for five of the six interviewees, there is a very serious concern that cracks are appearing in this integral dynamic, which is a theological, moral, spiritual, and (in a canonical sense) legal one between a bishop and his priest.

Each of the interviewees expressed grief in terms of depression and secondary trauma. They all displayed what American psychologist and author Dr J. W. Worden calls 'traumatic bereavement', that is, each interviewee expressed concern and a sense of loss both for a Church they thought they knew and a Church with which they were familiar and which they trusted.

Superordinate theme 3: Fear

Whilst this superordinate theme could be subsumed into the later superordinate theme of shame and isolation, it emerged as so important for the interviewees that it merited its own superordinate status. The fear described by the interviewees manifested itself, for the most part, in fear of false allegations. Their fear lay in the fact that they were vulnerable to false allegations being laid against them, due to either misinterpretation or vindictiveness. This fear was compounded by the further fear that they would be 'hung out to dry' by the bishops, even if the allegation was false or malicious. They feared that, given previous attempts by the bishops to protect the institution, the bishops would continue to do the same even if it meant some of their priests had to be sacrificed for the greater good. This fear, in turn, fed into other superordinate themes such as betrayal and questioning of the Church, both of which are explored further below.

> We need a bit more understanding. Priests need to know they are safe. It's caused an awful lot of fear. (Philip)

Fear for the future of the Church

> I'm just hoping and praying that there are no more accusations, or people finding things that have gone wrong in the past. (Christopher)

> We need more courage. Blow the insurers. We need to be radical. (Philip)

All of the interviewees spoke about how they believed their ministry within the Church meant they were members of a very well established and reputable institution whose future was never in doubt. The crisis in England and Wales, and indeed throughout the world, had arguably shaken the very foundations of the Catholic Church's credibility. Apart from the interviewee who was ordained after the crisis erupted, the other five reported that when they were first ordained they could never have imagined anything that would undermine the Church in such a profoundly damaging way. They spoke of concerns about the future of the Church; but they did not express doubt about its continuing existence in the future. They called for it to change, to be much more accountable than it has perhaps ever been. Interestingly, each interviewee described this potential for greater accountability as one of the very few positive things to come out of the crisis.

Fear of false allegations

Five of the six interviewees expressed concern and reported a degree of personal fallout as a result of the sexual abuse crisis in Ireland, and its inevitable accompanying publicity. They had friends who were priests in Ireland who reported feeling somewhat vulnerable and fearing that if an accusation were made against them they would be removed from their duties with great publicity, without due process and without a proper opportunity to defend their good name. Some Irish priests reported to the interviewees a feeling something akin to being 'cannon fodder'. The priests whom I interviewed were all unnerved that their fundamental right to be presumed innocent until proven guilty might be sacrificed in the same way that Church authorities appeared to sacrifice the rights of the alleged perpetrators. However, even priests who are guilty have rights and are entitled to due process.

The presumption of innocence underpins our state legal system, and associated with this presumption are the right of the accused to be made aware of an accusation and the fundamental legal principle *audi alteram par-*

tem—hear the other side.[2] The interviewees were not confident that these fundamental rights would be afforded them by the Church authorities. They also reported their disappointment that the secular world showed more concern for their well-being than their own bishops. Individual reactions varied from expressed concern through to developed fear.

> I am still a bit concerned about malicious allegations. (Christopher)

> I had a fear of being accused because of what some others did. (Christopher)

> It shocked, shocked me when people started being accused. (Gerald)

Fear of working with children

> I had a fear of being accused. I was frightened to be alone with a child in any circumstance. (Christopher)

> When I was first ordained it was good practice to pick children up and hold them. I wouldn't do it now. You'd be leaving yourself wide open. It would be inappropriate. (Daniel)

> I threatened to stop going into the school. The Head told me that if I withdrew completely the whole ethos of the school would change. It was wise counsel. I subsequently realised that he was correct; but I was still furious with the priest abuser. (Daniel)

> Some priests used the excuse that bishops would hang them out to dry if they were accused. Some priests think bishops assume you are guilty and you have to prove you are innocent. (Daniel) [Daniel was speaking about priests choosing not to minister to children]

It is important to note that the interviewees, with one exception, reported that they were not frightened of working with children; but they had become wary of how other adults would perceive their ministry with children in the light of adverse media coverage. The one priest who did not express this view explained that his lack of engagement with younger children was not a result of the scandal but simply recognition that this particular ministry was not his *forte*. I found it interesting to note that all of the interviewees expressed their confidence and gratitude to diocesan safeguarding commissions for their attempts to continue to foster their ministry with children. Whilst this is an encouraging and laudable position for the safeguarding commissions to take up, this does not negate the fact that the experience for all of the interviewees resulted in considerable distress.

Superordinate theme 4: Betrayal

Each of the interviewees reported concern about what they considered to be a degree of deception on the part of the bishops. For me as a researcher and as a brother priest, it is noteworthy to acknowledge that the sense of betrayal, in its many guises, had perhaps the most profoundly negative effect on my interviewees. Whilst none of the interviewees explicitly used the term 'friendly fire', the term suggests itself when we read the accounts of feelings of being betrayed on all levels listed below.

Betrayal by perpetrators

> Fury at priest abuser. (Daniel)

> It was a betrayal of trust. I couldn't comprehend it. Why would a priest take on such a role? It doesn't make sense. (Anthony)

I would've been quite happy if I'd found out that he'd topped himself, to be honest. Looking back, I suppose you shouldn't ever think like that of anybody. At the time, [it seemed] almost like this sort of Victorian morality—taking the honourable way out, although it wouldn't have been moral. (Daniel) [Daniel was referring to a predecessor who had been convicted of child sexual abuse]

It's completely incompatible. I couldn't get my head round it. Their whole life would be completely sordid. (Daniel)

Common to all interviewees was a reference to what they called 'the brotherhood of the priesthood'. However, each of the six interviewees expressed a feeling of betrayal by brother priests who had sexually abused children. As a researcher, and a brother priest, I found it interesting to note how each interviewee had conflicting feelings towards priests convicted of sexual abuse of children. As well as feeling betrayed, each described a feeling of bewilderment and each described the feeling of compassion for brother priests for whom their public ministry had ended. It was not just the fact that their brother priest's ministry had finished, it was the accompanying shame and scandal that they had to endure. This feeling of compassion, in turn, triggered a feeling of guilt by the interviewees since it seemed to undermine their standing as priests and their ability to continue to minister with integrity. This term bears further exploration since its impact has significant implications regarding how victims are viewed and dealt with. Unless this 'brotherhood' is fully understood, it is almost impossible to fully appreciate the dramatic effect it had on the interviewees. Having a sense of brotherhood brings with it the dangers of specialness and elitism, more commonly known as clericalism. This is a particularly thorny issue as it touches the core of the role of priests in the Catholic community and their identity. It has also been suggested that clericalism was a contributory factor to the culture in which abuse happened.

This has profound implications on the mindset of priests and their attitude and response to 'brother priests' who have sexually abused children. This can often take the form of misguided loyalty to a brotherhood which, instead of being inclusive, is in reality exclusive and is perceived as such by victims of clerical abuse. The irony is that a lack of concern for victims of clerical abuse is in fact a betrayal of 'the brotherhood of the priesthood' to which priests are all called by virtue of our baptism. The notion of a brotherhood of priests does not exclusively pertain to fellow ordained Roman Catholic priests. Baptism invites us to share in the priesthood of Christ. Thus any abuse of any member of the Church is a betrayal of the brotherhood of our common priesthood. It should be noted that all the interviewees viewed abuse by brother ordained priests as especially pronounced and hard to bear.

Betrayal by Church authorities (national and international)

> I would be one of those people who said there were two scandals. The way the Church behaved and is still behaving is wrong. It is still a scandal. (Gerald)

> There were several complaints about a priest, and bishops were reprehensibly moving them on. (Daniel)

> It appears they are more interested in the good name of the Church rather than care of individuals. (Anthony)

> Betrayal of Church authorities [is] harder to bear than initial scandal. (Matthew)

> Priests have no confidence in bishops. (Philip)

> The biggest shock was that the Church was concerned about its image rather than doing the right thing. (Gerald)

All of the interviewees reported that, as hard as it was to believe the initial abuse by priests, what was even more disappointing was the initial handling by the Church authorities, by which they meant the bishops both in England and Wales and indeed in any country where the scandal erupted. As can be seen by the quotations above, the interviewees were scandalised and embarrassed by what they described not merely as an inadequate response but a grossly unjust response. They reported that it left them not only disillusioned as members of the Church but also frustratingly in the position of trying to defend the indefensible. This fracture between the relationship of priests and their bishops is explored in greater detail below in the superordinate theme of the lack of confidence in the institutional Church as regards this issue.

Superordinate theme 5: Shame and isolation

All of the interviewees reported the toxic effect of the scandal and how it was handled by Church authorities. They described the regular experience of feeling ashamed about being a priest and struggled with how they believed they were perceived by the general public. For all of the interviewees, this was a unique experience in their priesthood which left them with a feeling of shame, despite their innocence, and a feeling of isolation because they did not believe there was anywhere they could process what they were going through.

Collectively branded

> Someone came to the door looking for money. When I refused he said, 'You're all a load of bloody child abusers'. (Christopher)

> You don't expect children to have the intellectual maturity to differentiate the difference between a good priest and a bad priest. It seemed that the kids in school had come to the conclusion that all priests were tarred with the same brush, which is sad. Initially I was very angry. (Daniel)

> Only very occasionally has someone said, 'You are all the same, you are all paedophiles'. That really hurt. (Gerald)

> In a way we are all being labelled. It's an undermining of the priesthood. (Philip)

> Friends think Catholic priest equals paedophile. (Philip)

All six interviewees reported that one of the most difficult things to bear about the fallout from the abuse crisis was what they perceived to be other people's perception of them. Several priests reported that the experience of priests being ridiculed by comedians was quite hard to bear. This experience was made worse when they were watching television with friends or family. They reported that they felt trapped because they did not feel that it was appropriate to profess their innocence. They also felt uncomfortable because they wondered what people, watching television with them, were thinking and whether they were embarrassed by it for different reasons. These feelings of embarrassment as a result of being collectively branded were common amongst the six priests despite their very varied ages and experiences. This seemed to compound their sense of injustice since in each instance none of the interviewees was guilty of any abuse.

Adverse media coverage

> The negative feedback is what's feeding society's perception of faith and religion. (Anthony)

> I still wonder if there's a concerted campaign in some quarters. There is certain anti-clericalism especially in Ireland. Clergy in Ireland were far too powerful. (Daniel)

> What makes me angry are the comments, the jokes. They diminish the Church and diminish peoples' opportunity to come to Christ. (Anthony)

The interviewees reported that they had become an easy target and akin to cannon fodder for anyone in the media who wanted to label all Catholic priests as potential child abusers. They each reported the difficulties they had endured with comedians taking what they described as cheap shots at priests in the Catholic Church. This experience in turn engendered a sense of anger at and betrayal by the tiny minority of priests who had abused children and exposed their brother priests to explicit derision. This situation was further exacerbated because the interviewees felt that they had no forum in which to defend themselves against assumptions pedalled by people in the media, whom they regarded as prejudiced.

Ridicule and humiliation

> I remembered jeers and sniggers and they used to spit on the back of my coat. Other priests who went into the school experienced similar things. I had been away for a month so didn't realise what had happened in my absence. (Daniel)

> Somebody came to the door begging for money. When I refused to give him some he shouted, 'You are all abusers'. I don't take much notice of someone who's coming to beg and doesn't get what they want. (Christopher)

All of the interviewees described at least one occasion in which they had to endure ridicule and abusive comments. Because of the humiliation attached to this particular scandal, the interviewees did not feel that they were in a position to defend themselves against people who were abusing them lest they fan the flames and get accused of denial and cover-up. This experience left them with a sense of helplessness and a notion that they had no other choice but simply to endure provocation for acts for which they were not responsible.

Stigma

> We are all suffering for all those who have done the abusing. (Christopher)

> The whole thing has undermined our integrity. (Philip)

> I used to be proud to be a priest, but I feel a bit wary about it now. (Christopher)

> I was almost ashamed to go out of the house with a collar on. (Philip)

> This guy was chaplain to a handicapped fellowship group. For the first time ever in my priesthood, I felt ashamed of being a priest; I didn't want to wear clerical dress ever again. (Daniel)

> When I hear about priests in the press I think: 'Oh, not again. I wonder how long ago was this one? Is it historical or something?' That's still going on;

> most of the time we've become a laughing stock.
> (Gerald)

All the interviewees reported a degree of concern about how they were perceived as priests. They each wrestled not merely with how they were perceived despite the fact that they had not committed any abuse, but also with their own perception of brother priests who had sexually abused children.

Superordinate theme 6: Impasse

The interviewees each described the tension between their core beliefs (including forgiveness, reconciliation, and the brotherhood of priests) and their responsibility as priests for the pastoral welfare of those on the margins of society, in this context the victims of child abuse. It is interesting to note that this was the only area in which they felt a sense of torn loyalties. Any disagreements or differences of opinion as regards dogma or practices of the institutional Church were reported as more of a cerebral tension rather than torn loyalties which affected the core of their identity.

Tension between reconciling clergy perpetrators and justice for victims

> This guy is my brother, so is this guy. (Matthew) [Matthew was referring to one of his brother priests who gave his life to save some children, and to another brother priest who was convicted of child sexual abuse.]

> I couldn't comprehend why a brother priest would do this. (Anthony)

> There's a real sadness about anyone in prison. (Philip)

> It's a chronic psychological complaint. If someone has offended once, they will do it again. In the past

we didn't realise that. We have been compromised
and handicapped because we emphasise forgiveness and reconciliation. (Daniel)

One feels that they should be given a chance to say
sorry. I don't know if they are. Perhaps more priests
were unjustly condemned. (Christopher)

It is difficult to untangle the torn loyalties the interviewees
shared as regards the victims themselves and their brother
priests who were perpetrators of child abuse. As the quotes
above suggest, the interviewees seemed to be trying to
process where their loyalty to their brother priests ended
and where they ought to hold their brother priests
accountable for their actions. Some of the interviewees
described the difficulty of having sympathy for brother
priests who had been imprisoned, with a notion that,
whilst their actions deserved imprisonment, their imprisonment in turn engendered a feeling of sympathy.

Lack of leadership from bishops

When I realised what had happened, I was disappointed—I'm trying to find a word that is stronger
than disappointed—I suppose shocked would
count. They have put the Church before the individual. (Anthony)

From the victim's point of view, it looks like these
priests are being kept and looked after. Where's
the justice? (Gerald)

To some victims it must seem like the priest got
away with it. (Gerald)

Throughout a priest's ministry, there will be many times
when he will look to his bishop for advice and guidance.
As far as the response to the child abuse crisis goes, all the
interviewees reported a lack of confidence not only in

initial reactions but also about how bishops would respond if the reputation of the Church came under threat. The notion of 'better for one man to die for the people' (Jn 18:14), whilst not explicitly referred to, was implied.

Superordinate theme 7: Lack of confidence in the institutional Church as regards this issue

It is a normal part of clergy life for a Catholic priest to question facets of Church teaching and organisation. In common with my own experiences in the priesthood, my interviewees saw as healthy a challenging search for a balance between Church teaching and the realities of day-to-day ministry. They displayed the same attitude to the implementation of teaching as the experience of people to whom they were sent to minister. However, in the context of this issue, questioning the Church was of a different magnitude. Rather than simply discussing and respectfully differing, the disagreements here generated a profound loss of confidence in the institutional Church which, in every other context, was their point of reference. This led them to, among other feelings, a sense of being abandoned.

Lack of openness and transparency

> I don't feel like I have a coping mechanism. This scandal shows up the infantilisation of priests and people. We need to grow up and have honest and adult relationships. (Philip)

> We need to talk about this in very explicit and practical terms. (Matthew)

> Priests can become too professional, in the wrong sense, not really engaging with people, just cele-

brating the sacraments. I think we're in danger of
becoming fundamentalists. (Daniel)

As previously noted in this chapter, each interviewee
reported divided loyalties between what they perceived as
their allegiance to brother priests and the anger they felt
toward and their sense of betrayal by the priest offenders
themselves. They reported that the actions of what they
described as a 'tiny minority' had seriously impinged upon
their own ministry and how they perceived they were
viewed by other people.

All six interviews expressed similar sentiments to Dr
Marie Keenan's 2012 finding that Irish priests were generally unaware of inappropriate behaviour by the 'tiny minority'. Experiences of priests in other parts of the world are
relevant to these findings since all six interviewees regard
the Church as one body. The participants felt a degree of
naïveté and embarrassment about what they now considered, in retrospect, to be blatantly obvious. When the
individual and institutional dimensions of the problem were
brought together, as they were by Dr Keenan, what became
evident was how the bishops, religious superiors, Catholic
laity, and the individual perpetrators were related in a web
of interacting dynamics and relationships that contributed
to the evolution and maintenance of the problem.

> There is a lot of fear and a lack of trust. I feel hurt
> by the attitude of priests towards their bishop.
> They have no confidence in them. (Philip)

> That was the biggest shock for me: that the Church
> was more concerned with its image than doing the
> right thing. (Gerald)

A recurring theme throughout the one-hour interviews
was a sense of disillusionment with how the priests
perceived themselves, how they felt they were perceived

by others, and how they in turn perceived their bishops. This subtheme overlaps with a sense of betrayal, a sense of lack of leadership and the loss of a moral compass.

Superordinate theme 8: Resilience and commitment

Having reflected on the experience of the interviews and their content with my supervisor Dr Ballinger, it occurred to me as the researcher that it was remarkable that all of the priests I interviewed were still in post. Given their reports of disillusionment with and betrayal by the Church authorities, none of the interviewees ever gave a hint that they had had enough and were going to resign. As their interviews progressed, several of the interviewees expressed compassion for their bishop, the same bishop who they earlier condemned for ineptitude. Each interviewee expressed continued commitment to offending priests, again in sharp contrast to the anger and sense of betrayal expressed early on in each of the interviews.

Their sense of commitment was both admirable and encouraging; it forced me to consider my own position in the Church as a fellow priest. I can concur that my own experience echoes those reported in these interviews. Despite feeling overwhelmed at times, each priest reported his determination to remain committed to his ministry as a priest serving what he described as an imperfect institution. To my surprise, not only as the researcher but also as a safeguarding trainer, each of the interviewees expressed a desire for more training about safeguarding. This contrasts sharply with evidence, albeit anecdotal, of priests refusing to engage with this training because they considered it to be too depressing.

Loyalty

> I'm 40 years a priest. I've always been positive and
> never consciously regretted my decision to be
> ordained. Sometimes I've thought sod this for a
> game of marbles. (Daniel)

> Perhaps one plus that's come from this terrible
> thing is that we don't feel so much up there.
> (Christopher)

> Where it always appeared that the Church was
> being harsh, now it can be appealed and reviewed
> and it makes you think hold on, there might be
> more to the story than I've been told. (Gerald)

I also found it interesting that, despite the reported frustra-
tion, despair, and betrayal, the anger that was expressed by
the six interviewees did not dominate their responses. They
each, in their own way, reported traumatic experiences of
being an innocent priest caught up in the child abuse crisis.
However, far from appearing to be consumed by what could
be considered to be justifiable anger, they instead displayed
compassion for all those involved in these scandals. Thus
it would seem that it was not a question of anger versus
compassion, but rather the case of the interviewees man-
aging to be angry whilst maintaining the ability and willingness to show compassion. They reported sympathy for
Church leaders and sympathy for offending priests and each
recognised the absence of malice on behalf of the bishops
on England and Wales. 'Wounded but still standing' is
perhaps the most accurate description of the priests who
were interviewed. This tension as regards anger at brother
priest offenders and the initial response by the bishops
seems contrary to the interviewee's expression of sympathy
for both offending priests and bishops. As a researcher, I
simply note this contradiction and I think it is indicative of

the fact that the interviewees were processing the effects of the scandal. I think that this process was developed and enriched by the experience of each interviewee of being interviewed and being allowed to talk openly and frankly for the first time about the effects of the scandal on their own priesthood.

None of the priests expressed any regrets about being a priest. Significantly, they also reported that their religious belief and their faith in the Church remained intact. At a human level this is quite remarkable. Another pleasant surprise for me as the researcher and fellow priest was the reported determination by each of the interviewees to make sure the child abuse crisis did not affect their future ministry with children, although they did mention a current degree of unease in conducting this part of their ministry. I must confess that, as the researcher, this was most unexpected. Added to this unexpected revelation was the discovery that all of the interviewees expressed gratitude for and confidence in the guidance given to them by each of their diocesan safeguarding commissions.

Tenacity

> If I was exonerated I'd be taken back by fellow clergy. None of this was even on my horizon before the explosion. (Daniel)

> They should have normal relationships with children, with women, with other men. You can be tactile and friendly when appropriate. A priest's house shouldn't be a place where he pulls up the drawbridge. (Daniel)

> People in the parish have contributed to my confidence. The parishioners, the parents seem to understand. That gives you a certain amount of confidence. (Christopher)

All six interviewees displayed remarkable tenacity. The experience of being an innocent priest in the midst of the scandal has had an exceptionally adverse and challenging effect on all six participants. They reported an experience which tainted the very core of their identity as members of the Church and as priests/office holders of the Church and their ongoing role within the institution. None of the priests interviewed seriously considered the possibility of leaving the priesthood or the Church. As a researcher, and a brother priest, I found this quite remarkable given the level of existential angst, betrayal, and abandonment that each interviewee, to a greater or lesser extent, reported. This might go some way to explain the extent of the damage done to priests against whom no concerns or allegations have been raised. For each of the interviewees, the priesthood was much more than either a job or a career; it was the essence of who they were. Whilst this sustained their loyalty to the Church, it also deepened the pain which they expressed. Their reaction to the betrayal by Church authorities was much more pronounced than the hurt they reported by being stigmatized by the media and society at large. As a fellow priest and therefore an insider researcher, I can empathise with their reaction to what seems like 'friendly fire'.

Forgiveness

> Whatever the public perception is, I have found the bishops to be good men, very mutually support-ive. All the bishops were very kind and genuine people; that's a very important thing to say. (Philip)

The findings illustrate the interviewees' extraordinary ability to hold on to and manage the tension between the profound anger they experienced and their capacity to show compassion. Also manifest amongst all interviewees was a similar ability and willingness to hold the tension between exasperation at Church authorities and a willingness to forgive and recognise their lack of malice.

Faith

> I'm confident that we wouldn't cover up a scandal again. I think the bishop would take appropriate action if an accusation was made. (Gerald)

> It's exceptionally horrific. I think the bishops' commitment is genuine. They are wanting to do the right thing ... by survivors, perpetrators, families, communities, everyone. (Philip)

> It doesn't seem to stop people coming into the Church, joining the Church. People have still got great confidence in the Church, also in the priest. (Christopher)

> I thought it had to be dealt with. I was given a terrific welcome. People here are very good to their priests. (Christopher)

> I've got confidence in myself, in other people interpreting what I do. I've been here and the people are gaining confidence in me. (Christopher)

> Ok, priests made mistakes and did wrong things, and perhaps that's what we've got to accept; but I am very optimistic and positive. (Christopher)

Despite the trauma, Matthew and his five brother priests revealed an exceptional depth of faith in their own ministry at that moment and for the future, in the resilience of their parishioners and in their own sustained and deeply held religious belief. Perhaps the experience of having for the first time a difficult conversation on this sensitive subject enabled each participant to voice their concerns and process the effects of the scandals. This process seems to have brought them back to a place where they can begin to revive their confidence in the future of the Church, despite its imperfections.

As the researcher, I simply note that the interviewees sometimes contradicted themselves and some of what they said was ambiguous. This does not cast doubt on the findings; rather, it more likely indicates the traumatic effect of the crisis and the difficulties the priests are still experiencing in processing its effects. It is also possible that they were developing their thoughts during the interviews because each of the priests reported that his discussion with me was the first time he had had the opportunity for a thorough, focused conversation about the subject and its effect on his life, his identity as a priest and his ministry. Each priest may well have been adjusting and nuancing his thinking as he formulated and then heard his own answers and interacted with me, the interviewer.

As Matthew said, 'We need to talk about it in very explicit and practical terms.'

Notes

1   In thematic analysis in psychology, a concept is a way to classify the world in your mind. The hierarchical model of concept classification includes three levels of concept: the most general is the superordinate concept, followed by the basic concept, and the most specific is the subordinate concept.

2   The Latin maxim *audi alteram partem*, one of the most cherished and sacrosanct principles of law, has evolved from three simple Latin words to mean that no person shall be condemned, punished or have any property or legal right compromised by a court of law without having heard that person. See *Duhaime's Law Dictionary*, 'Audi Alteram Partem Definition'. See also J. M. Kelly, 'Audi Alteram Partem; Note'. Natural Law Forum. Paper 84 (1964). http://scholarship.law.nd.edu/nd_naturallaw_forum/84.

4

CRISIS, BETRAYAL, AND A SENSE OF LOSS

T HE SERIOUSNESS OF the child sexual abuse cases for the Church, along with its paramount concerns for the children who were abused and for safeguarding those in its care, have overshadowed concerns for innocent priests. But the interviews with the six non-offending priests indicate that the scandals affected them psychologically as individuals and as office holders in the institution of the Roman Catholic Church, and therefore may also have produced similar issues for the many thousands of innocent priests whose lives have been deeply affected. The responses of the participants in this study demonstrate that their concerns have been exacerbated by a lack of attention from Church authorities. To avoid repeating the past error of focusing only on the effects on the Church as an institution, I will examine first the effects on non-offending priests as individuals, even though there is much overlap between personal and systemic issues, especially where the latter contribute to the former. I will then turn in the next chapter to the effects on the Church and its office holders.

Before analysing the interviews, however, I must acknowledge that there is considerable academic discussion among qualitative researchers about how to assess the validity of this type of psychological research. Four principles are sometimes used to evaluate it: sensitivity to context, commitment and rigour, transparency and coherence, impact and importance.[1]

To help to demonstrate sensitivity to the context of the six priests, I decided that it would be more appropriate to conduct the interviews in each interviewee's home or place of work. I felt this would in some way empower my interviewees since the interviews were taking place in familiar surroundings and my hope was that they would feel they 'owned the room' and thus were more likely to engage with the process without any fear of intimidation.

As regards to commitment and rigour, since I made the effort to visit my interviewees from as far afield as the southeast to the northeast of England, there could have been little doubt as to my commitment to the process. During the interview I made every effort to remain attentive and respectful and as such I am confident that my interviewees felt that they had been heard and that each of their contributions was invaluable. The rigour I applied was thorough in so far as each interview was recorded and later transcribed by an independent third party. The individual interviews took an average of six weeks to analyse.

Transparency and coherence can be evidenced by the clear stages of the research process. The superordinate themes reported by the individual interviewees correlated logically and I believe contradictions were identified and dealt with clearly. In order to ensure that my research data was valid and trustworthy, I kept a transparent 'trail' of each of the six interview processes. Thus from selection to final analysis each interview can be tracked to ensure validity.

Finally, the impact and importance of the findings was clear as each of the interviewees commented that this was the first opportunity that they had had to seriously and thoroughly discuss the impact that the child abuse scandal had had on their lives/priesthood. Whilst each interview was idiosyncratic, they shared a commonality as regards what I would describe as a cathartic experience which enabled them to voice previously unheard and unrecognised opinions and experiences. Another measure of impact and importance was the reaction of my brother priests to whom I reported the initial findings. To my surprise, there seemed to be an insatiable appetite for the information they heard. To date, every priest with whom I have shared some of the initial findings has voiced the opinion that this research into non-offending priests is long overdue.

Hearing the voices of non-offending priests

I am acutely aware that this is research done by a single insider researcher with priests who knew I was both a priest and a safeguarding specialist. Throughout the research process, I had to manage the tensions among my various roles, aided by regular and rigorous academic supervision. I am therefore confident that the data I have unearthed has real depth and richness. My role as a priest and safeguarding specialist helped to smooth our path through what were difficult and sensitive conversations for this group. Data from other studies could be different; but I remain confident the basic themes would remain.

I believe I have discovered what Revd. Professor Peter M. Gubi, a Professor of Counselling and Spiritual Accompaniment at the University of Chester and a deacon and presbyter of the Moravian Church, describes as the 'less-heard voices'.[2] All of my six interviewees, to the best of my knowledge, belonged to the vast majority of Catholic priests in England and Wales who are not accused nor convicted of any abuses against children. It is precisely because of this that I chose the qualitative methodology of interpretative phenomenological analysis in order to seek an insider's perspective.

I realize the potential dangers of making generalizations from such a small sample. However, the sample was intentionally small as it was not intended to be a basis for generalisations, but rather to illuminate in detail the experiences of non-offending Catholic priests who are still in ministry. However, from my experience and from the reactions of fellow priests with whom I have shared the rich responses in the interviews, the six interviewees seem to be typical in every way.

Their interviews produced results which were nearly unanimous and revealed superordinate themes which ran through their discussions with me: existential crisis, grief and loss, fear, betrayal, shame and isolation, impasse, lack of confidence in the institutional Church, and resilience and commitment. Only the most recently ordained priest did not feel a sense of existential crisis.

The feelings that they expressed ranged from being overwhelmed to losing their reference point. There were feelings of fear, betrayal, humiliation, tension, and disillusionment. On the other hand, feelings of loyalty, tenacity, forgiveness, and faith were enabling them to maintain their roles as priests. The study also revealed contradictions, ambiguities, and confusion. This likely demonstrates that the priests were still having difficulties in processing the effects of the trauma caused by the scandal.

If the experiences expressed to me by these six priests are representative of the Church generally, my research has revealed that this crisis has produced serious psychological effects on non-offending clergy and that the Church, nationally and internationally, has yet to recognise and deal with these effects. It has also still to face radical issues related to priests' role in ministry and their relations with their bishops.

There is strong evidence within this study of the stigma that non-offending priests still perceive that they have to endure, and these feelings are re-opened every time a new case comes to light, whether locally or in the international Church. This is something that all my six interviewees expressed. As I am writing this, the Royal Commission into Institutional Responses to Child Sexual Abuse in Australia is providing an example of this by shining yet more light on the terrible abuse allegedly committed by some Church leaders there. The public hearings are revealing some gut-wrenching personal accounts: stories of young people (and their families) crippled by sexual abuse; stories of utter betrayal; stories the Church would rather not hear but stories it must hear, even though they are stories that renew the stigma for innocent priests.

Psychological issues for priests

The scale of the crisis in the minds of the six priests is clearly reflected in the interviews. This can be seen, for example, in Matthew's use of the word 'holocaust'. The priests said that they at first found the accusations about clergy child sexual abuse unbelievable until they were overwhelmed by the sheer number of allegations. This points to the extent of the problem as revealed in the United States and Ireland especially.

The idea of holocaust communicates the scale of the crisis in the minds of the six priests, the number of victims, the suffering and the number of countries involved. The anger expressed by the priests echoes that found in Brid Fahey Bates' 2003 study of priests of the Rosminian Order, the Institute of Charity in Ireland. She researched the emotions which members experienced from cases against some members of the institute past and present and she recorded different forms of anger. Her findings bear a remarkable resemblance to my findings.

First, the anger that anyone would do something to discredit himself or the Church which Bates found was clearly reflected in my study, for example, in Daniel's observation: 'You come into a Church, assuming you trust in the Church and believe in the Church, and then somebody, not just anybody within the Church but a brother priest, offends in such an atrocious way.'

Then there was anger that all members are regarded as being guilty. A number of my interviewees used the phrase 'tarred with the same brush'. Daniel, for example, said: 'There was a lot in the media and press about paedophilia and it would seem that they had come to the conclusion that all priests were tarred with the same brush, which was just sad.'

Most of the priests I interviewed spoke about their early experiences of seminary formation. Those ordained before the abuse crisis spoke about the lack of human formation and the lack of room for emotional development. Speaking about his seminary rector in the 1960s, Philip said, 'He was living in the 1930s. So what we regarded as normal dialogue and conversation and questioning and all the rest of it, he regarded as insubordination.' Later in the interview he said that he emerged from the seminary at 24 years of age and was 'sheltered'. He added that 'there is an immaturity in us (priests) generally about lots of things'.

The language used by the priests in my study suggests that they felt traumatised by the crisis. Arguably, Catholic priests live with a certain set of assumptions about the Church and their fellow priests although there is a lack of research to identify these assumptions.

Religious and spiritual beliefs have been identified as having a central role in the meaning-making process because faith provides a unique framework to make sense of difficult times.[3] A religious belief system can be an unfailing way to make meaning of injustice, suffering and trauma that non-religious forms of coping cannot provide. However, as a researcher I find myself asking what happens when the religious institution to which one belongs and the religious belief of the person are the sources of the grief and trauma. As the researcher, this was a critical finding. I am absolutely convinced that this brings another dimension to the sense of trauma, one which has existential repercussions for all my interviewees. Philip, for example, asked, 'Where is God in all this?' This is a profound question and shows the depth to which this crisis has taken some priests in their reflection, faith and sense of self.

Amongst all the interviewees there was, to varying extents, a spiritual crisis which was exacerbated by the fact that the reference point for the expression of their spirituality, and indeed their core identity, was the primary cause of their spiritual crisis.

Shame, isolation, and a loss of identity

The six priests all spoke about the sense of shame they experienced as a result of the behaviour of the priests who abused, and the criticism directed at the Church as a result of the handling by bishops of allegations against abusers. The scale of abuses and the impact of personal stories of victims led to a feeling of being collectively branded by the media, commentators, citizens, and fellow Catholics. The Boston crisis of 2001, the Ryan and Murphy Reports of 2009, and individual cases in the UK or elsewhere involving sexual abuse by a Catholic priest, bishop, monk, or brother all lead to adverse media coverage and a recycling of old stories. Recent high-profile cases involving abuses by celebrities, while not directly implicating the Catholic Church, do little to reduce the sense of shame felt by these men as the issue continues to receive prominent media attention.

Shame is an emotion which involves an overall sense of being a bad person, with a global sense of being deficient, damaged, or lacking in worth. The natural shame reaction involves hiding from others. This can be seen in abuse cases where the accused covers his face to avoid meeting people or being seen face-to-face. It is understandable that priests, whose ministry involves working with people, and who are often in a prominent position, feel vulnerable and embarrassed by the media attention they experience in the abuse crisis.

American psychologist Dr J. P. Tangney contrasted the relationships between guilt and empathy and shame and empathy. She found that guilt and empathy 'go hand in hand'. Shame, on the other hand, appears to interfere or 'derail' the empathic processes. She writes that 'the shamed individual is inclined to focus on himself or herself, as opposed to the harmed other'.[4] These are important findings as they suggest that the shame priests are experiencing could have an inhibiting effect on their normal empathic response. In particular, it could lead to a lessening of empathy towards the victims of abuse, the very people who have been harmed most in this crisis.

The issue of clerical sexuality was a taboo area for most of these men's lives. Dr Marie Keenan writes that clerical sexuality in Ireland has been surrounded by a 'conspiracy of silence'.[5] It is arguable that the situation in England and Wales was not substantially different. Suddenly, as a result of the crisis, it became a matter of discussion and debate in the national media. Daniel, for example, said: 'Priests and paedophilia ... seem to be synonymous and I think we are an easy sort of target. It's very easy to say, "Well, you can't trust them on any of these moral issues because (a) they're celibate or (b) they're paedophiles" … And a lot of it is being perceived as being celibate is weird anyway.' Matthew said that 'the Church's teaching on sexuality in general, together with the child abuse scandal, just makes me very vulnerable because these are just incomprehensible to people'.

Philip spoke about being a 'convert' to the issue of clergy child sexual abuse. It is interesting that he used a religious image to communicate this change. This suggests a change of beliefs and values, and sums up the experience of other priests. The assumptive world of the priests, regarding the behaviour of priests, the support of bishops, and the regard of other people, has been changed profoundly and this was reflected in my interviews.

These changes can lead to what is known as 'ontological insecurity', where 'ontology' is related to the term 'being'. This term resonates with my interviews which revealed insecurity as regards the interviewees' core identity (superordinate 2).

The priests also spoke about a relationship of trust with the Church and Church leaders. Philip said he was 'very, very naïve' as a young man. Gerald described the Church as 'nurturing' and Daniel spoke of priests he knew as a child who were 'inspirational'. Matthew spoke about retreats where he could experience God in a personal way. Daniel agreed that he 'lived and breathed' the Church from an early age. The Church that was revealed in these quotations was one that inspired these men to dedicate their lives to the service of others and to make a promise or vow of celibacy. They immediately were given a place of esteem within the Catholic Church and society. Christopher said that when he was first ordained he felt 'very much put on a pedestal'. The abuse crisis, however, revealed things through the media that were 'horrific', 'sordid', harmful, scandalous, and embarrassing.

A number of the priests I interviewed spoke in ways that demonstrated that internal adjustments had taken place. Gerald said that during his formation he experienced the Church as 'powerful, structured, nurturing' and that he 'easily identified with the Church'. It was somewhere he belonged, a 'Catholic cocoon'. He referred to his shock at the number of abuse cases as the parish priest was the face of the institutional Church and that 'you then become the representative of a body which was deceptive'. He asked himself, 'How do you live with that?' He added that 'your position is untenable, in that you can't not be the parish priest'. These excerpts reveal that Gerald wrestled with his role and identity when faced with both the facts of what had happened and the reactions of other people. He moved to a point of hoping that people could still see good in the Church. He realised that in order to continue as a priest in the Church he had to accept the accusations made against it.

Grief and loss

The second superordinate theme which came out of my interviews was that all six felt grief and a sense of loss. This adversely affected the identity which they thought was theirs as priests, their respect for and confidence in the authority of the Church and at least some of the reference points which guided their lives.

The shock of the revelations led the participants to a reappraisal of the way that the Church authorities had handled such cases in the past. With the exception of Anthony, who was ordained after the abuse crisis became a focus of media attention, the other priests said that they had been unaware of such behaviour by priests. Christopher, for example, said that he was 'completely innocent of any thoughts that way'. The Nolan report and the Irish scandal led to a realisation that 'some terrible things' had gone on.

The Church they are part of has survived; but it is different in many ways so that aspects of that Church, and the ways of believing, thinking and acting that were part of it, have also been changed. In this context it is useful to explore models of grief and loss to help to understand the experiences of the priests.

Viewed as a whole, the superordinate themes found in the views of my interviewees have some similarity to the seven stages of grief listed, among others, by Elisabeth Kübler-Ross in her 1969 book *On Death and Dying*: shock, denial, anger, bargaining, depression, testing, and acceptance. These stages are different emotional states that people go through when facing traumas or significant life changes. The stages do not exactly match the experiences of the priests, and some stages resonate more than others.

Shock

While the six priests did not describe physical symptoms, all of them spoke in terms of the shock that they experienced as a result of the crisis. The sense of shock is communicated effectively in Christopher's response: 'I was shocked and annoyed when I heard what some priests had done. I couldn't believe it.'

Denial

All but one of the priests in this study said that their initial response to the crisis was denial. Daniel, when asked about his initial reactions in the mid-nineties on hearing the first reports of sexual abuse of children by priests, said, 'My initial reaction was denial, really. I thought well this must be some sort of anti-clericalist secularist thing to discredit the Church.'

It would not be accurate to say, however, that they continued to be in denial about the crisis at the time of the interviews. It seems that the priests had passed through this stage and no longer denied that abuse had taken place or the scale of it. They also, for the most part, no longer tried to defend the response of the bishops and religious leaders. The one exception was Anthony, the most recently ordained, who took a more sympathetic view of the good intentions and poor responses of the bishops. Interestingly, all of the interviewees acknowledged that their initial response was denial; but it seemed to me that what they were referring to was more akin to disbelief than denial.

All six priests acknowledged that there had been denial by the Church as an institution, which was reflected in the response of bishops and the avoidance of any discussion or training about the issue of child sexual abuse by clergy. Gerald, for example, commenting on the Church in Ireland, said, 'I still feel that the Church's reaction ... or solution to the Irish situation seems to be "well, if people were more prayerful, if priests were separated in training it would all go away". It still seems to be completely naïve.' This suggests that he thinks the Church is still in denial about aspects of the crisis and its implications. The interviewees also said that they avoided talking about it in sermons and did not discuss it with parishioners. All six priests were clear that the Church could not go on as before.

Anger

The focus of the anger varied for each of the priests, with considerable overlap: anger at the priests who had abused, anger at bishops for their poor response, and anger over betraying the Church, the victims, innocent priests and priests who had been accused or found guilty of abuse.

They were also angry at the media for the way priests were presented, especially by comedians on television.

Bargaining

The priests spoke of their appreciation of the safeguarding measures being put in place in dioceses, even though the measures had affected their ministries. Daniel spoke about a 'loss of spontaneity', and this is reflected in the responses of other priests who spoke about the way they had changed their behaviour in some circumstances, especially regarding their ministry with children. The policies, reports, and safeguarding procedures could be interpreted as a response of the Church as an institution in order to be seen to be dealing with the scandal in an appropriate way, so that it could then return to its work as a Church and retain the structures as they were before. Christopher, for example, spoke about the paramountcy principle—contained in the UK Children's Act of 1989 and adopted as national policy by the Catholic Church in England and Wales in 2001—as a burden, but could see that it enabled him to continue with his ministry. Other priests echoed similar sentiments.

Depression

This stage can last for extended periods and can be debilitating. It can include believing that nothing good will ever happen again and rebuffing all attempts to find constructive solutions. As far as I could determine, however, none of the priests I interviewed was suffering from depression in a clinical sense, though all reported what might be described as 'low spirits'. This can be seen in their use of words and phrases such as: 'perplexed', 'uncomfortable', 'the damage it had done', 'coping with', 'undermining', 'upsetting', 'unease', 'sadness', 'drained', 'deadening

effect', and 'insecurity'. It can also be seen in their comments on the damage to the Church's reputation and on
the effect on the relationship between priests and bishops.

Testing

The sixth stage involves looking for ways to change
thinking to lift the depression. The priests come across as
what Irish social researcher John Weafer, among others,
calls pastoral pragmatists.[6] They all spoke about how they
had adjusted their pastoral practice so they were not alone
with children, were more cautious in social situations and
used the diocesan safeguarding commission, brother
priests, or friends to know how best to deal with specific
situations. In that sense there was evidence of 'testing' out
how best to adjust their pastoral work in the light of the
scandal without compromising their ministry as priests.
Matthew, for example, talking about his own practice, said,
'There are things that I wouldn't do now that I might have
done previously in terms of socializing with students.'
Daniel spoke about a situation, responded very carefully
and wondered if he was being overly cautious.

All the priests spoke about ways that they were more
aware of safeguarding issues and did not want to put
themselves in situations where there could even be an
appearance of inappropriate behaviour. They spoke about
being cautious, using common sense, being more aware;
they provided specific circumstances where they had
consulted friends, parents, teachers or safeguarding officers to be sure about how to proceed. The priests were
clearly going through a stage of testing new ways of
understanding and behaviour in order to protect children,
but also to protect themselves from the possibility of a
false allegation.

Acceptance

The final stage of grieving involves actively moving forward to deal creatively with future needs. The priests in the study expressed anger, sadness, disappointment, shock, and betrayal; but they also demonstrated a sense of accommodation with what had happened in the positive sense of wanting to move on with their pastoral work. There was a level of acceptance about what had happened. Regarding the Church, which he had criticised for its poor response, Gerald said, 'Even the institutional Church that, as you say, I represent, there is good in it.' They all continued their pastoral work, albeit with adjustments to their behaviour in the light of new policies and procedures.

Grief, the personal experience of a loss or significant change, can also be described in terms of tasks rather than stages, as does American psychologist Dr J. William Worden. People do not engage with or complete the tasks in any particular order because 'each person's grief is like all other people's grief; each person's grief is like some other person's grief; and each person's grief is like no other person's grief'.[7]

The tasks relate to the loss of a loved one; but they can be adapted to understand the loss and grieving of the priests in this study, who are all deeply committed to and 'love' the Church. The priests spoke of their loss of a former identity as priests, the loss of focus and authority, their loss of confidence in the institutional Church and the loss of a reference point in their lives and work as priests. Worden proposes four tasks of grieving.

To accept the reality of the loss

This can be seen in the way the priests spoke about moving from their initial denial of the first accusations to the impossibility of denying what had taken place. Philip, for

example, said, 'I just thought, you know, this is all unreal.'
He goes on to report how changes occurred: 'And I just
remember how it changed a very easy relationship ... with
schools in particular ... but everywhere really. They were
suddenly very aware.' Gerald said that he realised that the
Church was 'into self-preservation'.

Worden requires an emotional acceptance of the loss.
In Philip's case, the emotional acceptance came through
his personal experience of listening to a victim of abuse in
a particularly horrific and unsettling case. Philip said, 'I
suppose that was really my first direct experience of it, and
I just hadn't any notion of it and of the depth of the
destructiveness of it ... So of course, then in a sense, I'm
almost a convert.'

Worden notes that traditional rituals can help people
to move towards acceptance. None of the priests men-
tioned a parish, deanery, or diocesan liturgy or meeting
being organised to help the priests to acknowledge the
impact of the abuse and the feelings involved.

Worden makes it clear that not everyone experiences
grief in the same way. This can be seen in the responses
of the six priests in this study. Those who, like Philip, had
personally met victims seemed to be affected more profoundly than others. The priest who was most recently
ordained, Anthony, appeared less affected than the priests
who had been in ministry for some time. But all of the
priests in this study spoke of some degree of upset or
distress. This may reflect personality differences as much
as anything else.

Work through the pain of grief

It appeared that the six priests were struggling to come to
terms with the pain, grief and other emotions they experienced as a result of the loss. As Worden identifies, a
person's experience of loss leads to an insecure attachment

to or conflicted relationship with that which was lost. In this situation, the insecure attachment affected their relationship to the Church as an institution and their particular diocese as a specific part of their day-to-day lives. This particular superordinate theme is complicated because each interviewee retained both common and individual responses to the crisis.

Adjust to an environment in which changes are in place

All the priests spoke about how they had adjusted their pastoral practice as a result of the revelations of abuse, the changed perceptions of lay people and the media, and new policies and procedures. Anthony, for example, said that the crisis had not changed the way he did things, as seminary had prepared him for this new reality. At the same time, he said he had thought how best to manage confessional practice, where a priest would himself be alone with a child. The old Church had gone for these men, with the assumptions, securities, and blind spots that were part of it, and the priests now operated with more awareness. There was loss involved in this, particularly the loss of a certain freedom in ministry. Philip referred to being cautious in the playground with children, and Christopher said that he stopped taking the altar servers to McDonald's as a treat once a year. He spoke about being 'quite wary about children'.

To find an enduring connection to the old while embarking on a new life

All of my interviewees expressed a sense of grief and loss over a Church with which they felt familiar but which had now been undermined. The priests who were interviewed continued to be priests in good standing with their dioceses or religious orders. In a sense, their whole life required a continued connection to the Church, which was also the source of their suffering. The priests did not embark on a new life; it might be more accurate to say that they continued with their chosen life but with new awareness and changed perspectives of themselves, the Church as an institution and of the world where they worked and ministered.

A distinctive feature of Worden's model of grieving, which is particularly relevant to priests, is his identification of the spiritual task of grieving. American Dominican priest and author T. P. Doyle notes his loss was fundamentally spiritual in nature.[8] Worden explains this in terms of meaning-making. He suggests that, in order to move on from the loss and grief, a person has to construct a new understanding of reality that acknowledges the loss and creates a new meaning structure which includes the loss but is not defined or paralysed by it. He writes: 'Most people ... usually decide that they must fill the roles to which they are unaccustomed, develop skills they never had and move forward with a reassessed sense of themselves and the world'.[9] We have seen this in the way priests have had to implement safeguarding policies and practices, make adjustments to pastoral practice in their work with children and discuss with colleagues, family and friends appropriate behaviour in certain circumstances.

The trauma which Doyle explores could not be recognised until he was able to connect with his denial and his dependence on the Church system for security. He echoed my own experience of interviewing the six priests who described the Church as their past, present, and future. My interviewees found it hard to reconcile the responses of the Church leadership with the official teachings of the Church. Philip, for example, asked if the Church culture prized integrity as much as it should and if 'there isn't an awkwardness and a straightforwardness and an honesty that we need to have'. Implicitly, he is acknowledging these things are lacking in the Church as an institution. Similarly, Anthony said, 'The Church has made some rather silly and naïve decisions.'

Secondary victims

In her identification of the colleagues of offending priests as secondary victims[10], Dr Joanne Greer mainly recognised two groups of priests: those who had a personal relationship with an abuser priest and those who were directly affected by one. She focused, for example, on non-offending priests who were trained by the same formation staff as an offending priest and so could begin to distrust their own formation and therefore their ability to minister. Non-offending priests who knew an offending priest personally could feel guilt that they had not reached out to him more or in a way that would have prevented him from abusing.

She also listed as secondary victims those non-offending priests who had been confronted and vilified personally by those who had been abused, priests who had lost financial and moral support from their congregations because of the demands of abusive priests, and priests who had seen parishes cut back or closed due to scandals.

Three of the six priests I interviewed did not fit into either group. Of the remaining three, Daniel took over a parish from an abuser priest and Philip had met victims; but neither reported any adverse experiences as a result. Matthew was the only one who knew an offending priest and reported being deeply disturbed by his case. But while none of the six spoke of themselves as victims, all displayed many of the same symptoms as Dr Greer saw in the groups of priests and others whom she identified as secondary victims.

As with Dr Greer's secondary victims, all of my interviewees expressed anger at the abusers who they saw as betraying them and the Church, yet they also expressed concern for the treatment of offending priests. Their feelings of shame and humiliation at being unfairly branded as abusers are similar to the feeling of an innocent priest who is unfairly personally attacked by a victim. The distrust of the formation process and difficulties in accepting the responses by some bishops and religious leaders who seek to deny or cover up accusations are characteristics which my interviewees share with Dr Greer's secondary victims.

The other negative effects revealed in my interviews with the non-offending priests—the existential crisis, grief and loss, fear, shame, impasse—coupled with the fact that half of them exhibited the same effects without any direct contact with the scandals, indicate that this may be a more far-reaching issue for the Roman Catholic clergy, one not limited to non-offending clergy who come into direct contact with the scandals.

Moving forward

It is clear from the interviews that all of the priests had a profound sense of loyalty to the Church. They are all, to the best of my knowledge, still in ministry. They have overcome their initial disbelief, have read the reports, watched television programmes, and endured the mockery of comedians and rejection from some people. Yet they still continue to function as priests in the Church in a range of settings. They speak of finding forgiveness for the perpetrators, and of the need for the Church to extend its care to them. Many said that they felt more confident now as a result of improvements in safeguarding policies and practices, and as a result of the positive response of friends, families, parishioners, and fellow priests. In itself this is a remarkable story of faith, tenacity and resilience.

> I've got confidence in myself, and in other people interpreting what I do. I've been here and the people are gaining confidence in me. (Christopher)

> It's exceptionally horrific. I think the bishops' commitment is genuine. They are wanting to do the right thing ... by survivors, perpetrators, families, communities, everyone. (Philip)

They exhibited feelings of shock, shame, sadness, anger, and fear. These are considered as negative emotions, and they tend towards behaviours which are designed to protect the self. Focusing on one specific action or response often does this, for example, when experiencing fear the person feels an urge to fight or escape. If the person feels angry, it suggests that a boundary has been crossed and the anger response is a way to communicate this to the other person. It has been suggested that sadness leads to the person retreating within themselves to regroup in order to adjust to loss before being able to pick up their lives and move on as normal.

These negative emotions are balanced by 'positive emotions'. American psychologist Barbara Fredrickson explains that whilst negative emotions narrow a person's thought and focus (to fight, flight, or freeze, whichever seems most beneficial for survival), positive emotions have a potential to broaden a person's thoughts and perspectives. For her, positive emotions have the potential to restore flexible thinking.[11]

The interviewees discussed serious issues, yet there was often humour and shared appreciation of an amusing comment or anecdote when talking to these priests. They were focused and had moved to a place where they were able to continue with their ministry in a positive way with support from inside and outside the Church. This social support is a valuable resource which enabled them to remain resilient in the face of the enormity of what had happened.

If, as Fredrickson proposes, the fostering of positive emotions is related to how people construe personal 'meaning', then religion is ideally placed to provide a meaning structure for people, in both ordinary events in life and major life changes. Worden has related the task of grieving to spirituality. He suggests that spirituality for the grieving involves finding meaning in the loss. Fredrickson's theory is a valuable resource when we consider how to respond, for example through therapy, to any non-offending priest. Geary and Greer challenge the Church, as a grieving community, to put aside its disillusionment and accept the task before it without flinching.[12] It appears that the priests I interviewed have resources they can call on to face this challenge.

Notes

[1]   See, for example: J. A. Smith, et al., *Interpretative Phenomenological Analysis: Theory, Method and Research* (London: Sage Publications, 2009); R. Elliot, et al., 'Evolving guidelines for publication of qualitative research studies in psychological and related fields' in *British Journal of Clinical Psychology* 38/3 (1999), pp. 215–229; L. Yardley, 'Dilemmas in qualitative health research' in *Psychology and Health* 15(2) (2000), pp. 215–228; L. Yardley, 'Demonstrating validity in qualitative psychology' in *Qualitative Psychology: A Practical Guide to Methods,* 2nd ed, (London: Sage Publications, 2008), pp. 235–251; or J. A. Smith, 'Evaluating the contribution of interpretative phenomenological analysis' in *Health Psychology Review* 5/1 (2011), pp. 9–27. The evaluation principles are discussed by Yardley and Smith.

[2]   P. M. Gubi, *Listening to Less-Heard Voices: Developing Counsellors' Awareness* (Chester: University of Chester Press, 2015).

[3]   M. B. Werdel and R. J. Wicks, *Primer on Posttraumatic Growth:*

An Introduction and Guide (Hoboken, NJ, USA: John Wiley & Sons, 2012).

4   J. P. Tangney, 'Self-relevant emotions' in *Handbook of Self and Identity* (New York: Guilford Press, 2003), pp. 384–400.

5   M. Keenan, *Child Sexual Abuse and the Catholic Church: Gender, Power, and Organizational Culture* (New York: Oxford University Press, 2011), p. 30.

6   J. A. Weafer, *Thirty-three Good Men: Celibacy, Obedience and Identity. A Sociological Study of the Lived Experience of Irish Diocesan Priests in Modern Ireland, 1960-2010* (Dublin: The Columba Press, 2014).

7   J. W. Worden, *Grief Counselling and Grief Therapy: A Handbook for the Mental Health Practitioner*, 4th ed, (Hove, SXE, UK: Routledge, 2010).

8   T. P. Doyle, 'The spiritual trauma experienced by victims of sexual abuse by Catholic clergy', *Pastoral Psychology* 58/3 (2009), pp. 239–260.

9   Worden, *Grief Counselling and Grief Therapy, p. 35.*

10   J. M. Greer, 'Secondary victims in a sexual abuse scandal' presentation to the *Safeguarding Children and Young People Conference*, Marist Brothers General House, Rome, March 2012.

11   B. Fredrickson, 'The role of positive emotions in positive psychology', *The American Psychologist* 56/3 (2001), pp. 218–226.

12   B. Geary and J. M. Greer (eds), *The Dark Night of the Catholic Church* (Stowmarket, SFK, UK: Kevin Mayhew, 2011), pp. 585–590.

5

CHANGING RELATIONSHIPS WITHIN THE CHURCH: A TIME FOR DIFFICULT CONVERSATIONS

I N MY EXPERIENCE of three decades as a priest, the community of priests is regarded as a brotherhood with a significant place in the Church; this is a place which, from the perspectives of the priests I interviewed, is being significantly affected by the scandal. Such was the depth of the feeling of betrayal expressed by the priests over the Church's handling of abuse cases that Gerald, for example, described it as an additional scandal. Not only did they see their place in the world as under siege, but their attitudes toward the Church as an institution and to its hierarchy, especially bishops, were also severely shaken.

The place of the brotherhood

By virtue of baptism people become members of the 'family' of the Church, an image extended by the image of the 'mother Church' and God the 'father'. Ordination into the priesthood is an invitation into the 'brotherhood of the priesthood', an ontological and thus irreversible change.

In her 2011 study of nine offending clerics in Ireland, Dr Marie Keenan noted that from the early 1960s to the early 1990s, the period in which those priests were abusing children, priests were presumed to be superior to laity and as such formed an elite within the Church. The clergy offenders understood themselves as set apart as 'God's men on earth' and behaved accordingly. The priests I interviewed saw this not only as a betrayal of the trust of their victims but also a betrayal of the trust of their brother priests who would have to bear the stigma of 'Roman Catholic priest equals paedophile'.

Speaking of a priest who had abused, Daniel said, 'I also felt he'd betrayed us—the other priests he worked with.' Gerald, speaking about priests who had abused said, 'I feel that they've brought a lot of good people into disrepute.' It is understandable that priests feel betrayed by men who were committed to the same life and ministry and who had behaved in ways that undermined the ministry of others and appeared to tarnish their work. Philip was particularly upset as there was a sacrilegious element involved in a story of abuse that he recounted. This abuse of the sacraments was something that he described as evil and, in that sense, represented a betrayal of all of his values as a priest.

The clerical ethos created a culture of entitlement to respect from the laity for simply being a priest. Above priests, however, the hierarchical system of the Church and loyalty to this hierarchy, in place since the first century, creates the opposite culture: members who are expected to do what they are told and go where they are sent. As Rev. Derek Smyth, a Dublin priest and a former Director of the Emmanuel House human skills training centre in the US, has noted, dissent is perceived as intolerable betrayal.[1] This hierarchical system is still very much in evidence. Priests often have little or no say in the major decisions that affect their lives. A possible consequence of this dysfunctionality is arrested development.

There is a view among priests that suggests that we are now in an era when the trickle-down theology of the experts is giving way to the 'percolating-up' theology of the 'People of God'. This mindset, if lived out, radically challenges the notion of the brotherhood of priests as an elite club and begins to encourage and enable priests, whether offenders or not, to perceive victims primarily as equals.

As a long-serving priest and, in this case, an insider-researcher, I have seen that in most areas priests have highly tuned and effective social skills. Their role demands considerable competence and ability. However as a researcher and a therapist, I see arrested psychosexual development as contributing to the clergy's response to this very difficult scandal.

The hierarchical nature of the Church means that addressing the contribution of the clerical culture to the scandal can only come from the top down. Those who challenge the institution can find themselves isolated and deserted by those from whom they would like support. My interviewees reported that they felt overwhelmed when new allegations emerged in the media.

The more I reflected on what the interviewees shared, the more I saw unanimous gratitude for being allowed to have a conversation about such a critical issue. Each participant acknowledged the Church had finally begun to react appropriately and had introduced robust safe-guarding policies and procedures. Each of the interviewees appreciated the opportunity to share their experience of being innocent priests in the shadow of this scandal. As Philip said: 'It's just horrendous; I have never spoken to anyone about this.'

The importance of facilitating difficult conversations

This positive reaction of the priests to the interviews has been one of the outcomes of this study. It created a space where they could share their feelings about the crisis and have their feelings heard and respected in a non-judgmental way. This issue bears direct relevance to the experience reported by the interviewees.

From a counselling perspective, the effects of a well-conducted qualitative interview or conversation can give the participants new insight into the topic. We find examples of this understanding in the comments of some of the priests who were part of this study. Matthew expressed the 'need to talk about this in very explicit and practical terms', while Anthony admitted that he 'sometimes [felt] inadequate, despite the training'. Daniel said priests, as men, should be more 'in touch with their emotions'.

A related issue is the capacity of priests to have adult conversations with their bishops, especially about issues which are taboo and therefore difficult. As far as I know, at the time of this study none of the bishops of England and Wales had called the priests of his diocese together to a meeting with a facilitator to explore issues related to the abuse crisis, or about sexuality and celibate priesthood. In other countries there have been workshops or speakers have addressed priests as Dr Robert Wicks addressed Boston priests and Fr Timothy Radcliffe, OP, a highly regarded priest and speaker, spoke to the priests of Dublin. Archbishop Gerhard Ludwig Müller, prefect of the Congregation for the Doctrine of the Faith in Vatican City, spoke to the priests of Motherwell diocese in Scotland after the scandal involving the reports of sexual behaviour and the 2013 resignation of Cardinal Keith O'Brien. But nowhere, to my knowledge, has a diocese called priests together to reflect, discuss, and dialogue with the leadership about the abuse, its implications, and the consequences for priests and for their relationship with their bishop.

Irish researcher John Weafer notes that priests who speak candidly to bishops are often seen to suffer for their honesty.[2] Daniel quoted another priest as saying 'that's typical of bishops. They don't want to know you if they think they are going to hear something they don't want to hear or would be uncomfortable to hear. And if anything happened to you they would hang you out to dry.'

According to Weafer, bishops have various ways of 'punishing' priests, from appointing them to unattractive parishes (especially financially) to keeping them on the margins of the diocese. Writing of younger priests, he comments:

> Some of them said they are frustrated by the lack of consultation and domineering attitude of their superiors. Typically, they are appointed to their parishes by bishops, without consultation, and they are expected to obey their parish priests.[3]

Weafer quoted one curate as saying that it is never wise to challenge your bishop in public as 'it will be noted'.[4] He said that most priests acted out of fear and had learned discretion. He goes on to say that, although they are afraid of confronting their bishops because of possible consequences, the priests of all ages develop a certain independence of action in their own parishes.

> My research suggests that while Irish diocesan priests are constrained in many ways by a highly structured and strictly hierarchical Church, they also have the capacity to think and act relatively independently in certain circumstances.[5]

While priests have learned a certain pastoral pragmatism in their parish work, Weafer writes that there is a danger of a kind of developmental splitting, where they act as adults in their parishes and children with their bishop. One priest in his study said:

> In my experience bishops have very poor people-management skills and guys get hurt when wrong

decisions are made because the proper conversation never happens.[6]

It is reasonable to conclude from Weafer's research, the results of the interviews with the six priests who participated in my research and my own anecdotal evidence amongst priests, that there is still not a healthy culture of adult conversations between many priests and their bishops. Philip, for example, said that in the past priests were expected to conform. He said, 'I think things ought to be a lot more open' and that 'there was a lack of trust in the bishop'. He added, 'I think that's where we have got to grow up a bit in our relationships ... the honesty thing ... We ought to be able to have an adult relationship.' Philip is voicing the experience of many priests and he reflects the research undertaken by Weafer.

My interviewees traced these concerns back to what they expressed as their anger about the limitations of their formation programmes which they tended to attribute to the 'system' and the Church culture at that time. All of them recommended more emphasis on human and psychosexual formation. This was not simply as a response to the scandals, but rather as a way to better prepare priests to live healthy lives and to function effectively and securely in ministry.

If conversations are integral to our perception of reality, then the concept of difficult conversations becomes even more important since not engaging in such conversations might mean missing the opportunity to engage with an aspect of reality which is challenging. They might be the key to experiencing a reality without which we will remain at least partly in the dark. Safeguarding is such an issue: it can never be woven into the infrastructure of the Church, nor be an integral part of a priest's ministry with children, without facilitating difficult conversations. There was some acknowledgement in my interviews that their in-built inability to hold difficult conversations about certain issues also has also affected bishops. Daniel's sympathetic response, 'we were all taken in', shows priests experienced anger but also understood the difficulties bishops often faced when dealing with these situations.

Priests and bishops

Their anger at the 'system' for not preparing them to deal with certain difficult subjects was part of the wider anger felt by my interviewees who resented bishops and religious superiors who were aware of priests who were sexually abusing children but who, at least in initial responses to allegations, sought to cover them up instead of acting. This failure of leadership caused Matthew, for example, refer-ring to his elderly mother who lived in Ireland, to say:

> My lovely old mammy is over there trying to process this stuff ... She is just stunned, you know, that the bishops have been lying and people are fed up with this, and ... priests seem to be still okay in her eyes. It's the failure of the bishops.

The priests in my study demonstrated anger against bishops but not against the UK government, apart from Daniel who sensed that the state authorities and the bishop were taken in by the perpetrator to whom he referred. This is unlike Ireland where there was anger at bishops and at the Irish government for letting things get out of hand without owning up to their responsibilities.[7] To understand better my interviewees' depth of feeling about the bishops' handling of the clergy child sex abuse scandal, it is illuminating first to examine briefly how bishops and religious superiors mishandled allegations sufficiently for their actions to be elevated to a scandal equal to or surpassing the original scandal.

The 2010 John Jay Report identified five factors contributing to the American Church's mishandling of sexual abuse. These factors appear throughout the global situation and they were, to varying degrees, well known by my interviewees:

- failure by the Church leadership to recognize the seriousness of the problem
- overemphasis on trying to avoid a scandal
- use of unqualified treatment centres
- misguided willingness to forgive
- insufficient accountability

The clergy sex abuse crisis was portrayed as a 'crisis of ecclesial leadership' on the part of the bishops as endless media reports of clergy abuse and its mishandling sparked public outcries for greater transparency and accountability in the Church. Researcher Dr Marie Keenan specifically refers to priests' feelings of not being consulted, and how this contributed to low morale, something I was to find amongst all my interviewees. However, previous concerns for innocent priests focused more on giving them a greater role organisationally than on resolving their personal conflicts. She captures the systemic aspect of this dysfunctionality when she writes:

> Whilst the issues are complex, it is my view that the structures and systems of authority and power relations within the Church have allowed this secrecy and lack of openness and consultation to thrive. For many people it is the landscape against which much abuse including sexual abuse becomes possible.[8]

Dr Keenan reports from her study of priest offenders in Ireland that not only did Church leaders there fail to fully engage or deal adequately with offending clergy, but they also failed to undertake a comprehensive analysis of the problem. She reports that each bishop or religious superior seemed to adopt a defensive position in relation to either his diocese or his religious order and that the cases took place in an environment of the abuse of power and privilege.[9]

The issue of priests becoming 'operational casualties' of false or unproven allegations because of the defensive attitudes of bishops and religious superiors has also been reported and was expressed in my interviews.

One analysis concludes that the scandals have fundamentally changed the relationship of trust built on an ongoing dialogue between bishop and priest. This is similar to Dr Joanne Greer's observation that non-offending priests who have a direct relationship with an offending priest can find that their beliefs about 'how things are' and 'who is good' and 'what is right' in the Church structure are affected.[10] The damage done not just by complaints but also by how some priests have been treated by their superiors means that, in my experience in England and Wales and in my interviews, priests' confidence in their superiors could be described as shaky.

The sense of shock and disappointment at the response of the bishops was clearly seen among the priests I interviewed, whose views were all similar to Anthony's:

> When I realised what had happened I was disappointed, I'm trying to find a word that is stronger than disappointed; I suppose shocked would count. They have put the Church before the individual.

The issue of secrecy and 'cover-ups' has been part of the discourse related to this crisis. The review board in the United States and the Murphy Report in Ireland both note that bishops often appeared to have been chosen more for their orthodoxy than their management skills. While orthodoxy is desirable from a theological and moral perspective, it can be the antithesis of the very foundations of safeguarding. In these cases, it led to secrecy, lack of consultation, and the concentration of power in a small number of clergy. This stance is in stark contrast to the UK Nolan Report's call for 'openness and transparency'.

This resonated with the six interviewees who saw the bishops' approach and Church policy as betrayal, the fourth superordinate theme. Anthony spoke of priority being given to 'the good name of the Church rather than care of individuals', while Gerald went further to say the 'biggest shock was that the Church was concerned about its image rather than doing the right thing'. Matthew found that the 'betrayal of Church authorities is harder to bear than the initial scandal'. Philip said he thought that 'priests have no confidence in bishops'.

The priests spoke about the need for change in the Church. Gerald, for example, said, 'So, in a sense, I can say I belong to that institution and would like to see it change.' Daniel said that 'it made me question the institution'. Philip spoke about 'awkwardness', a lack of 'straightforwardness' and a need for 'honesty' in the Church. Matthew referred explicitly to a 'cover-up' when he spoke about 'the failures of leadership'. Later in his interview he referred to 'the silencing of the victims', which he found 'appalling'. He also referred to a culture that allowed this evil to flourish and spoke about the need for a culture of 'truth-telling' to replace secrecy and silence. Gerald described the way the institutional Church had behaved and is behaving as wrong.

Referring to earlier decisions by bishops, Anthony, who was inclined to give the bishops the benefit of the doubt

('Please God our bishops are holy men'), spoke about some 'silly and naïve decisions', which 'at the time ... were probably prudent'. Prudence suggests a tendency to be cautious and to withhold information rather than share it. He said he was 'disappointed' but did not use the word 'anger' or related words.

The priests gave the impression that they had moved from a Church where they felt secure and safe to one where they had to be careful about their behaviour and how others might interpret their behaviour. They could not take the bishop's support for granted and would be more vulnerable if faced with an accusation.

Gerald revealed a lot of processing regarding self-identity and his relationship with the Church. He struggled with the question about how to be the public face of the Church, maintaining his own integrity while acknowledging the failings of the institution. He suggested that all of this was necessary in order to have a new sense of self and to retain credibility with parishioners and the public. The other priests spoke about similar issues. Philip, for example, spoke about the move away from conformity in all aspects of priestly life. This suggests a new relationship between priests and their bishops, and their accepted role in the Church.

Psychologist Dr William Worden suggests that part of the task of adjusting to a loss or significant change requires spiritual adjustments which relate to one's values, beliefs, and assumptions about the world. The priests noted a level of hostility against the Church, particularly from the media and comedians but also from children. Gerald said priests had become a 'laughing stock'. Daniel said some of the bishops were just like lawyers, who now assumed that a priest was guilty and that the priest had to prove his innocence. Gerald spoke about needing to watch his own back and the institution's back. Philip spoke about having had a juvenile relationship with his bishop when he was first ordained and about 'having to grow up a bit'.

Allaying their fears

The six priests who were interviewed revealed three fears as a result of the crisis: a fear of working with children, which was the initial motivation for this research; a fear for the Church, which they are part of and love; and a fear of false allegations.

The Catholic Church has a network of schools across England and Wales. Priests, in their role as chaplains, would have been welcome visitors to schools and were (and are) often called upon to lead masses and other liturgies. Many parishes have youth clubs, groups of young altar servers, youth events such as pilgrimages and social gatherings, and, in recent years, many young people have participated in World Youth Day, a biennial gathering of young adults from the Catholic Church throughout the world. Priests acted as role models and sources of authority, often as mentors, in the lives of young people. This study demonstrates that the crisis may have had a damaging effect on this part of pastoral work of the Catholic Church. Christopher, for example, was still visiting primary schools and families, but was more cautious as a result of the crisis. Matthew, who did not work pastorally with children at the time, said that he would be more careful and attentive to things. Safeguarding officers may be at pains to indicate how to work safely with young people; however, the combination of policies and protocols, which appear to cast suspicion over priests, and the feeling priests now have of a lack of freedom and creativity in their work with young people seem to have created a climate which is undermining priests' ability to work with young parishioners.

Significantly, stories of false allegations and the way that priests are treated when an allegation is made against them have affected the priests deeply. In accounts by two priests who were accused in the course of their ministry, both speak openly about the necessity for protocols, even regarding investigations into priests who are accused. Both, however, feel that they had been badly treated by their bishops in the course of the investigation and, after being cleared, were hurt that the bishop would not write to their parishes saying that they had been found 'innocent'.[11] This accusation leaves a stain on the priests' life and ministry.

Priests, including those I interviewed, who are aware of such stories are understandably afraid of the possibility of an accusation against them. No doubt there are priests who look back on behaviours and activities with young people which may have appeared innocent at the time— youth events, parish outings, sports matches, or holidays— but which can be viewed differently in the light of recent allegations and convictions. Policies and practices were not the same when some of these men were young ordained priests working with young people.

The relevance of all the cited data from Weafer is its extraordinary similarity to that reported by my six interviewees and their mistrust of bishops. The priests I interviewed said how unhelpful the lack of dialogue with bishops was. The purpose of the data from Weafer is to provide the context for my conclusions about the importance of healthy adult development in priests in order to have adult conversations with their bishop without fear.

The well-being of priests

My experience of working with priests as the safeguarding co-ordinator for the Diocese of Salford had led to my concern for the ability of priests to be confident in their ministry with children. My initial research confirmed that the taboo of child sexual abuse was having such a negative effect on some priests that it effectively undermined their ministry with children. My impression was that some priests had become more cautious in their behaviour, some avoided being with children, and some felt paralysed regarding how best to respond. The threat posed by the fear of being accused of inappropriate behaviour and possibly of abuse had left them not knowing what to do or how to respond in pastoral situations. This led to a broader concern for their well-being as Roman Catholic priests who had not been accused of inappropriate sexual behaviour towards children.

The Church had betrayed its work with those on the margins of society by being exposed for oppressing the vulnerable. The Murphy Report had explicitly referred to the greater concern of Church authorities for the protection of accused priests and brothers and the Church's assets and reputation than for the care of the victims. This betrayal reportedly affected the perception of the Church by priests and laity, their confidence in the hierarchy, and the perception of the Church as a place of care and trustworthiness. Irish author John O'Donohue sums up the consequences of this perceived betrayal:

> Then the utterly unthinkable: the explosion in the sanctuary. A psychic bomb went off, a bomb that had been unknowingly assembled for years from materials produced by the denial of the feminine, enforced celibacy, power, loneliness, and sublimated politics of desperation.[12]

My analysis of the subsequent interviews with the six priests identified eight superordinate themes (crisis, grief and loss, fear, betrayal, shame and isolation, impasse, questioning the church, and resilience and commitment) along with a number of other significant topics which revealed undesirable psychological effects on them as non-offending priests. These themes and additional topics recognize that this is a multidimensional crisis which has evoked strong feelings of grief and a sense of loss. This research has identified or reinforced ways to help both innocent priests and the Church to move forward from this scandal.

Bishop Eamonn Walsh, then Auxiliary Bishop of Dublin, has acknowledged that bishops have a very serious obligation towards victims of alleged abuse; but they must not respond in a manner that might be unjust to the alleged abuser.[13] He urged a commitment to regular reviews of guidelines and best practices in this area. Bishop Walsh noted continuing great concern among priests over the process of being stood down from ministry when allegations are made, the manner in which parishioners are informed, and the provision of appropriate accommodation and support. Walsh further stated that if a priest is found guilty and permanently removed from priestly ministry, the minimum requirement of any bishop is that the priest be treated with respect and compassion. If this is adhered to, it will have a profound effect on the wellbeing and personal and institutional confidence of priests against whom no allegations have been made.

Notes

[1]   D. Smyth, 'The land of the pirates—Clerical culture and sexual abuse', *The Furrow*, 60/9 (2009), pp. 471–474.

[2]   J. A. Weafer, *Thirty-three Good Men: Celibacy, Obedience and Identity. A Sociological Study of the Lived Experience of Irish Diocesan Priests in Modern Ireland, 1960-2010* (Dublin: The Columba Press, 2014).

[3]   *Ibid.*, p. 217.

4   *Ibid.*, p. 217.
5   *Ibid.*, p. 217.
6   *Ibid.*, p. 172.
7   B. Fahey Bates, *The Institute of Charity: Rosminians, Their Irish Storey 1860-2003* (Dublin: Ashfield Press, 2003).
8   M. Keenan, *Child Sexual Abuse and the Catholic Church: Gender, Power, and Organizational Culture* (New York: Oxford University Press, 2011), p. 602.
9   *Ibid.*, pp. 273 and 598.
10 J. M. Greer, 'Secondary victims in a sexual abuse scandal' presentation to the *Safeguarding Children and Young People Conference*, Marist Brothers General House, Rome, March 2012.
11 Weafer, *Thirty-Three Good Men*, pp. 150, 154 and 165–167.
12 J. O'Donohue, 'Before the dawn I begot you', *The Furrow*, 57/9 (2006), p. 464.
13 E. Walsh, 'The relationship between bishop and priest', in *Priesthood Today: Ministry in a Changing Church* (Dublin: Veritas, 2014), pp. 275–283.

6

HEARING THE VOICES OF PRIESTS

THE ROMAN CATHOLIC Church globally and in England and Wales in particular has gone to great lengths to institute policies and practices to protect children and vulnerable adults from sexual abuse by anyone including the clergy and to begin to restore its good name which has been tarnished by these scandals. Within the policy guidance laid down by the Vatican for the Church in all countries, the Church's Bishops' Conference of England and Wales has used its internal autonomy to reform its safeguarding procedures to such an extent that it is now at the forefront of standards of child protection policies and procedures in the country: its 2008 national safeguarding structures, the establishment of the Catholic Office for the Protection of Children and Vulnerable Adults, child protection systems in every diocese, and its arrangements for congregations to join with either regional religious commissions or with the local diocese. Its policies and procedures are now appropriately linked to new UK government arrangements for wider child protection.

It has joined with and, in some respects leads, initiatives by the British government and especially its Safeguarding Authority, other faith communities, and agencies such as the Manchester Safeguarding Children Board in ensuring the protection of children and vulnerable adults. As noted in a mission to identify ways to ensure that Catholics and the Church were portrayed appropriately in the media when Pope Benedict visited the UK in 2010, the British government now recommends the Catholic Church policies and procedures to other institutions as a model to follow.[1] This is something I can attest to personally as both a priest and a counsellor of victims of clergy sexual abuse. This significant change in the Church's response should not be overlooked.

While all six interviewees acknowledged that the bishops of England and Wales have made significant strides in responding to the clergy abuse crisis, some of their statements indicate the reforms are not totally understood by non-offending priests. For example, a number of interviewees said that any accusation of sexual abuse meant that their priesthood was finished. Not only is this contrary to the Church's national policies and procedures, but I know that only accusations that have been sustained have resulted in laicisation. I was torn between being frustrated at their lack of understanding about such a vital topic and their lack of training, about which they each expressed concern.

Weaknesses in their understanding may be because the reforms have been under-reported by both secular and religious media, and because the Church may need to do more to reach its priests. To the extent that it may be representative of the Catholic clergy generally, my research has found that this is far from the only area in which more needs to be done for non-offending priests. It has also found that all non-offending priests, not just those with a direct link to an offender, are bearing burdens associated with other groups of secondary victims.

I am convinced that the findings from this study demonstrate that adopting a qualitative methodology has produced results that may have been missed by other methodological tools. My focus was on conducting and analysing qualitative semi-structured interviews using interpretative phenomenological analysis and hermeneutics. My position as an insider researcher, a priest with additional safeguarding experience interviewing brother priests, successfully complemented my chosen methodologies to enable this research to obtain what seem to be full and frank revelations from priests on a previously undiscussed taboo subject. The priests said how much they valued their research interview as it provided the first forum to reflect on the crisis and to think about it in a meaningful way.

For the priests in this study, and probably for those throughout the Church, considerable work remains to be done to repair relations between clergy and laity. They said they still lack confidence in dealing with minors and with the decline in their reputation with the public. It will perhaps be many years before priests feel confident to associate with children and young people to the extent that they enjoyed prior to the sex abuse scandal.

One of my primary concerns is the reported poor or complete lack of communication between the six interviewees and their bishop/superior. The six also found it difficult to comprehend how Church authorities could allow abusing priests to profess repentance only to continue their activities when re-assigned by their trusting bishop or religious superior. One of the recurring superordinate themes from the interviews pertained to the priests' lack of confidence in the culture of the institutional Church because of its response to the sexual abuse crisis.

One theme that emerged was the deep bond of brotherhood that is present among priests. My interviewees expressed no doubt that priests who sexually abuse children betray a sacred trust. But they also felt that the men who had behaved so appallingly should receive treatment and support.

All the six interviewees reported that the scandalous behaviour of some in the clergy caused them great anxiety and disturbed them both spiritually and theologically. They said their main challenge was trying to find forgiveness for the perpetrators against whom they also felt outrage, disgust, and betrayal.

The impact on non-offending Catholic priests in England and Wales caused by the sexual abuse of minors by a few in the clergy can be summarised very succinctly in the eight emerging superordinate themes. The priests whom I interviewed revealed an Existential Crisis in their sense of priesthood and ministry and in their own identity. They also experienced Grief and Loss. Also, there were feelings of Fear, Betrayal, Shame and Isolation. Five of the six interviewees felt that there was a lack of connection between their experiences and views and the official stance of the Church. This led to a feeling of Impasse and then to a lack of Confidence in the Church related to this issue. Despite these experiences, the interviewees demonstrated a personal Resilience and an enduring commitment to the Church. As the researcher, as well as an insider, for me the overwhelming impact of the various scandals and the way they were managed by Church authorities was the feeling of betrayal that all six interviewees said they experienced. Whilst feelings of having been shamed and let down by their brother priests and the anger against these perpetrators were manifest, the feeling of being betrayed by both national and international Church authorities caused the deepest wound. Thus at one level a sense of betrayal was both a superordinate theme in its own right and a recurring aspect of all the other superordinate themes.

Recommendations for change

The proposals in this chapter could assist the Church and its clergy to deal with this aspect of the crisis if the experiences of the priests I interviewed are common to those whose group is subjected to this type of scandal. They could be useful as well for other faiths and for non-religious organizations such as those in education and childcare because the incidence of child sex abuse in the United Kingdom and around the world is alarmingly high and is by no means confined to the Roman Catholic Church. Recently, the Methodist Church in Britain made a public apology after an independent investigation unearthed nearly 2,000 cases of reported abuse dating back to the 1950s. Two hundred allegations involved Methodist ministers.

Rev. Dr Martyn Atkins, General Secretary of the Methodist Conference, said in a statement:

> On behalf of the Methodist Church in Britain I want to express an unreserved apology for the failure of its current and earlier processes fully to protect children, young people and adults from physical and sexual abuse inflicted by some ministers.[2]

His statement reflects my view and the view of the priests in this study that co-ordination, co-operation, openness and transparency are the most effective tools available to address and to respond to this crisis. The only responsible course of action is to forge strong links with all organisations responsible for addressing this particularly difficult subject. This has proved to be especially true for the Roman Catholic Church in England and Wales, whose original 'in-house' response of avoiding publicity and the criminal courts system proved painfully inappropriate and inadequate.

Challenges for the Catholic Church

For any culture to survive in an institution, many in the institution have to support it, explicitly or implicitly, actively or passively. Even now it is, in my view as a long-serving priest, still very difficult for anyone in the Catholic Church to find the courage to accuse a priest of abuse. Bishops' Conferences and civilian authorities did not respond well to the accusations that were made, as the 2009 Ryan and Murphy Reports found in Ireland. These reports were also known to my six interviewees who expressed concern about the Church's response and its collusion with other Irish authorities.

All large institutions develop mechanisms of defensiveness. However, one unusual element in life in the Church makes its defensive mechanisms even more damaging: the Church controls the training of its leaders. In my experience, seminaries can produce dedicated, devout, and wise men; but the system can have an intrinsic bias towards conformity and against challenging authority. The monastic proverb 'Keep the Rule and the Rule will keep you' is in my view often translated into 'Keep the rules of this seminary and you will get ordained'.

This is a very dangerous pattern for a role in life. Unthinking obedience and loyalty can be a way to avoid pain and the tension of disagreement. This can be especially attractive if conformity means avoiding confronting those with arbitrary powers to appoint and promote. But it also involves compromise: stepping back from struggling with the Gospel-truth which is always greater than any institution.

But the damage may potentially be more extensive because being dominated in a system that requires, or is perceived to require, obedience can lead to a subservient and docile priest becoming domineering and uncompromising when placed in authority.[3]

In exploring how the priest-bishop tension has contributed to the crisis, Dr Marie Keenan identifies an unhealthy dynamic that appears to lie at the heart of the experience of diocesan priesthood: how to be an adult in a system that rewards dependent and collusive behaviour.[4] John Weafer reports that the majority of priests said that seminary did not prepare them well for life as an adult.[5] The same comments came from the priests I interviewed, such as Philip who said that 'it was very much a matter of keeping the rules and all that sort of stuff'.

These observations indicate a need for a model of human development for priests which takes account of their promise of obedience. Ronald Fairbairn, a Scottish psychoanalytic thinker, proposes an elegantly simple model of human development which takes account of the human propensity to become stuck in dependent relationships. Fairbairn proposes that we move from the absolute dependence of infancy, through the quasi-independence of adolescence, to the mature interdependence of adulthood. Infantile dependence is clearly not a healthy place to be for an adult, yet the descriptions of some of the behaviours of some priests seems to fit his description. As an analysis of Fairbairn's theory notes:

> The state of mature dependence implies a recognition of the separateness of individuals, even while they are involved in the most intimate and interdependent of relationships. Separateness thus in no way implies isolation, or even disconnection. Rather, separateness hinges on the recognition of the existence of the selfhood of the other ... It should be clear that perhaps the most salient practical touchstone for this sort of separateness will be the recognition and acceptance of individual responsibility.[6]

The pastorally pragmatic priests described by Weafer—those who try to 'keep their heads down' but who are somewhat afraid of their superiors—appear to have established a way of acting that reflects quasi-independence. They have not achieved true selfhood and do not develop responsibility for themselves in their relationship with their bishop. They relate to their bishop in terms of his role and not as a person 'who is in a role'. Mature interdependence requires a capacity to behave in an adult way, and to engage in adult conversations with peers and those in authority, respectful of their role but not losing a sense of self and autonomy in the process. This also requires a similar capacity and skill among the bishops.

The role of the bishop is critical. Many bishops could be appointed because of their ability as administrators or due to the fact that their orthodoxy makes them a 'safe pair of hands'.[7] The reality seems to be that many bishops have found themselves out of their depth when dealing with child abuse. One of the significant superordinate themes to emerge from my six interviews was the lack of confidence in the competence of their bishop and the institutional Church to respond appropriately to the abuse crisis.

I also share Keenan's concern for the lack of participation in decisions by those who ought to have been consulted. The lack of consultation between bishops and priests in this scandal has been presented in this study as a very serious situation which should be corrected.

In the past, it seems that some bishops and religious superiors sought to protect the institution of the Church by minimizing overwhelming evidence of abuse. This approach was further compounded by the reaction of some bishops to all of their priests. [8]

The clerical abuse scandal wrought great damage on American churches and above all the Catholic Church.

My six interviewees were all well aware of this fact. Where responsibility is denied for the behaviour of priests who molest children, the resulting feeling of demoralisation reported by non-offending priests is understandable and predictable.[9] Perhaps the confidence of non-offending priests in the institutional Church and its bishops and religious superiors will only be restored when they are given assurances that this will never happen again.

Changing attitudes

If a married couple use contraception, they're complicit in evil. If a priest molests a child, he gets a new parish. Indeed, sex itself seems to be in the cardinals' minds entirely an abstraction. It's a sin or an act rather than a relationship.[10]

During my decade as a Safeguarding Co-ordinator, I witnessed a significant change in the Catholic Church's mind-set from denial and a reluctance to acknowledge or engage with the scandal, to a willingness and ability to acknowledge, engage with and make significant contributions to the promotion of the welfare of the child as paramount.

Bishop Charles Scicluna was unambiguous in advocating this new mind-set at a 2003 conference in the Vatican. He stated that sexual abuse of minors by clerics is and always has been a serious violation of the Christian ethos and a tragic wound against the Church. This wound had also affected the well-being of non-offending priests. The bishop cited St Matthew's Gospel and the words of Jesus Christ concerning the scandal:

> If any one of you put a stumbling block (scandal)
> before one of these little ones who believe in me,
> it would be better for you if a great millstone were
> fastened around your neck and you were drowned
> in the depth of the sea. Woe to the world because

of stumbling blocks [scandals]! Occasions for
stumbling are bound to come; but woe to the one
by whom the stumbling block comes! (Mt 18:6–7.)[11]

He declared that the scandal is a tragic wound to all
members of the Church, clerical and lay:

Whenever a cleric, whether bishop, priest, or
deacon, sexually abuses a minor, a tragic wound is
inflicted on the Church. Such conduct is reproach-
able on various counts:

1. It inflicts untold damage to the normal sexual
    development, self-esteem and human dignity of
    the minor concerned;

2. It is a cause of scandal to Christians and non-
    Christians alike, a stumbling-block on many a
    pilgrim's progress in faith;

3. It invariably constitutes an abuse and a betrayal
    of the sacred trust which the People of God
    rightly have of their shepherds;

4. It damages the credibility of the Church and
    taints the beauty of Her testimony to the Gospel
    of Jesus Christ who is the Way, the Truth and the
    Life;

5. It discredits the ministerial priesthood and puts
    countless innocent clerics under the shadow of
    delinquency, crime and misdemeanour.[12]

He added:

The Church will address the established occurrence of sexual abuse of [a] minor by a cleric in
terms of working for the healing of [the] victim and
the just punishment of the cleric. The well-being
of the minor who has fallen victim to sexual abuse
by a cleric is to be of paramount concern to the
Church. Whenever possible, therapy should be

> offered to the offending cleric; but this does not exhaust the demands of justice. Penal procedures and disciplinary actions should foster and promote the common good. They should, as canon 1341 of the Code of Canon Law says, repair the scandal, restore justice and reform the offender.[13]

For many years, members of my faith community, especially my brother priests, have held a mistaken view: this new emphasis on the child and the resulting child protection policies were seen as meaning they could not perform their gospel imperative of ministering to children. They were not regarded as policies to ensure they could perform this duty with pride.

The six priests I interviewed by and large found the safeguarding policies and procedures, the Safeguarding Co-ordinator in their diocese and the safeguarding commissions to be very valuable resources and a welcome proactive move away from handling the problem discreetly, avoiding contact with police, minimising contact with victims or their families, moving the priest, or sending him for treatment and then reappointing him (if possible) to a new parish.[14]

As someone who has worked as a safeguarding priest, I can report that without exception each victim wanted recognition of what had happened to them and, if possible, an apology. Sometimes bishops were informed by their legal advisors to protect the institution and its assets by not admitting anything, not meeting victims, not accepting responsibility, and never apologising. This unhelpful stance is now staunchly resisted by the Catholic Safeguarding Advisory Service (the national advisory office for England and Wales) and by most key workers serving the Church in safeguarding.

However, the crisis is not over and the six priests interviewed for this thesis may only ever be confident once the bishops ensure that allegations are never again swept under the carpet. It seems evident that there is still a lot of healing and bridge-building to be done between bishops and their non-offending priests.

Weafer, in his sociological study of the lived experience of Irish diocesan priests in modern Ireland from 1960 to 2010, confirms the data from this research that priests in England and Wales do not have a good relationship with their bishop. Weafer reports that everyone he interviewed acknowledged that the relationship they had with their bishop is an unequal one. He cites one priest who was convinced that mandatory celibacy existed to make it easier to control priests. He quotes another priest who said:

> Even if you get a parish you don't want, you could say to the bishop that you will be back in six or seven years for another parish. There is almost always a Plan B, which the bishop would be willing to consider if he asked.

Weafer's observations are further evidence of the need for adult conversations between priests and their bishop.[15]

Little acknowledgment or provision of therapeutic intervention was offered to any of the priests I interviewed. Their sense of betrayal was manifest: betrayal by their offending brother priests and betrayal by their Church in how it dealt with sexual abuse by clergy.

In contrast to the interviewees' sense of betrayal, on 2 May 2015 *The Tablet* published an article by Cardinal Cormac Murphy O'Connor, the retired Catholic Archbishop of Westminster and former Chair of the Bishops' Conference of England and Wales. He pointed out that, at the time of his appointment to Westminster Diocese in February 2000, the abuse crisis had already inflicted terrible damage on the credibility of the Church. He admitted that when some victims and survivors had had the courage to come forward, they had not been listened to, or worse, believed. He added that in the forefront of his mind is the care of the priests of the diocese. He stated that he wanted any priest to feel able to come and talk to him. This is a desirable approach; but it is in stark contrast to the experiences reported by all six interviewees as regards their bishop or superior.

Bishop Eamonn Walsh states that the bishop/priest relationship exists on two levels: a one-to-one level and a group level. Both are important and the relationship is incomplete if one level is preferred to another. Both bishop and priest must engage with it, work on it, and nurture it. Walsh is clear that bishops must respect a priest's contribution and he cites the importance of this mutual support by quoting the Vatican II Decree on the Pastoral Office of the Bishops in the Church:

> To ensure an increasing effective apostolate, the bishop should be willing to engage in dialogue with his priests, individually and collectively, not merely occasionally but if possible regularly.[16]

Walsh adds that a bishop should have an open-door policy and direct phone line for his priests, with the understanding that a priest may have access to his bishop at all times. This would help to create an atmosphere which means a priest can easily arrange an informal meeting with his bishop. All of this is founded on a deep respect and indeed love for every priest in the diocese.[17]

Mgr Dr S. J. Rossetti urges bishops to affirm their priests, and to be encouraged to know that the great majority of priests in the US support and respect their bishop.

Although many observers assume that relationships between bishops and priests have been fatally ruptured, three-quarters of priests in the United States say they have a good relationship with their bishop and approve of his leadership.[18]

It remains to be seen whether bishops are able to provide the support that innocent priests need.

The best policy for bishops may consist of humility, caution and a determination to listen and learn. As American Roman Catholic priest, sociologist, and writer Rev. Andrew Greeley points out, they must also acknowledge that they made a terrible mistake in covering up sexual abuse by priests and then re-assigning the abusers.[19]

Beginning difficult conversations

The value in being able to talk about their issues which was expressed by the priests in my interviews raises the issue of the responsibility of those in authority to create opportunities for discussion, conversation and possibly counselling for priests affected by this crisis.

Priests, unlike other professionals, are not required to undertake continuing professional development, regular professional supervision, or any performance assessment. Spiritual Directors and regular attendance at the Sacrament of Reconciliation (confession) are at the discretion of each priest. In my experience, many therefore live and work alone, often even without any effective peer support or with only superficial peer relationships which can neither affirm nor challenge their ministerial practice or their way of living as priests. Isolation can be profoundly detrimental to a person, and I have seen in my former role as a diocesan safeguarding co-ordinator from 2001 to 2012 that it has potential implications for inappropriate behaviour and helps to establish the environment in which abuse is perpetrated. In my view, this dynamic does not cause but might well contribute to offending behaviour; either way, this way of living and working ought to be challenged.

Feelings on the part of the six priests such as shame, isolation, humiliation, and betrayal persist and are difficult components of an even wider difficult issue which all need to be addressed by the Church and by them as individual priests. They could be common among Catholic clergy and could also be experienced by other professions facing similar scandals. These feelings could be addressed in counselling arranged either within the Church or with external therapists.

It is therefore important that bishops and religious superiors offer therapeutic intervention to their non-offending clergy. They should open a dialogue between themselves and their priests and facilitate peer dialogue and support.

My experience with my six interviewees has led to my concluding that addressing this issue must take account of the concept of 'stuckness' in therapy. This is especially true in dealing with an underlying issue for non-offending priests: How to give them the confidence to have difficult conversations?

Priests may become stuck for different reasons, such as an inability to grasp a concept, an unwillingness to confront unwelcome changes, or facing too much change too fast. It may not be clear if they are indeed stuck, how and why they are stuck, whether it matters that they are having trouble processing, and, if so, how they can be helped to move on.[20]

Difficulties in addressing such problems can very often be rooted in the fact that somebody is stuck in the process, be it a therapist, a counsellor, a researcher, or an interviewer. Sometimes people can get stuck because the initial insight has been too rapid and too profound. There was much evidence in my findings of the necessity to pause in order for the priests to process what had happened as they reported continuing shock, a loss of their core identities as priests, disillusionment, and a loss of their reference point.

There were signs of another potential source of 'stuckness' for non-offending priests: the realization that there is no going back and they are heading towards considerable unalterable life changes. The interviewees reported feeling overwhelmed by the process. While there was no suggestion that they were resisting the changes in child protection and in their role and position in the Church, they repeatedly expressed a realisation that they were having trouble adapting and the Church was not providing help.

The extent to which non-offending priests are given permission to participate and encouraged to do so honestly and openly is particularly important. This willingness to question, and to be allowed to question, must include not just myths, taboos, and uncomfortable topics, but also presumptions and ways of thinking about these issues and 'taken for granted' certainties. It is necessary to begin the process of challenging areas where thinking has become somewhat lazy and confused. This must be part of a life-long strategy to constantly challenge and be open, especially about subjects that are most uncomfortable. The responses of the six priests indicate this may be a problem among priests in general and one which the Church is not recognizing or addressing.

The Church could also devise liturgies that address those caught up in such situations. The Archdiocese of Dublin, for example, held a service of lament in February 2011. As part of the Toward Healing and Renewal Symposium held at the Pontifical Gregorian University in Rome in February 2012, there was a penitential liturgy at which Cardinal Marc Ouellet, Prefect for the Congregation for

Bishops, presided. These liturgies demonstrate acceptance of the facts of abuse, show remorse, ask for forgiveness from victims, and create a space for healing, reconciliation, and forgiveness. They often involve significant and powerful symbolic gestures, such as presenting each participant with a small vial of healing oil.

Rituals can also enable others in the Church to process their feelings. One priest, for example, who had abused children said that Pope Benedict XVI's meeting with victims of clergy sexual abuse in Sydney, Australia, was a healing moment as he could now express sorrow to his own victims (personal sharing). Such events could help priests to process their feelings about their loss and the grief they experience.

The frank contributions of my six interviewees to knowledge about the effects of abuse, or similar trauma, could assist all therapists to devise appropriate counselling.

Treatment of offending priests

Priest abusers betrayed some of the most vulnerable members of the Church both criminally and immorally. The phenomenon and extent of clergy sexual abuse of minors may not yet be fully understood. There are estimates that child abusers in general commit about 60 offences for every case that surfaces and that the average abusing priest abuses 285 times. If these figures are even close to reality, for me as a researcher it raises the question of how much of the current crisis remains under the surface, despite the comparatively low number of officially recognized offending priests.

The six priests who were interviewed were aware that a few of their fellow priests broke the sacred bond of their calling. One referred to the fact that some of the abuse took place on Lindisfarne, 'Holy Island', and another referred to the abuse of the sacrament of Eucharist as part of the abuse. Despite these observations and the strong feelings they aroused in the interviews, there was a concern that abusing priests should receive treatment. There was also a concern expressed by some of the interviewees that the Church's response has moved from denial to a punitive stance towards those who have abused. My interviews revealed concern about what happens to priests who are dismissed from the clerical state.

According to canon 384 of the 1983 Code of Canon Law:

> [The bishop] is to have a special concern for the priests, to whom he is to listen as his helpers and counsellors. He is to defend their rights and ensure that they fulfil the obligations proper to their state. He is to see that they have the means and the institutions needed for the development of their spiritual and intellectual life. He is to ensure that they are provided with adequate means of livelihood and social welfare, in accordance with the law.

Even if a priest is found guilty of abuse, his bishop/religious superior therefore has responsibility for his welfare for life. This fact was something the six interviewees found reassuring, despite voicing their experience of being betrayed by priests who abuse children.

At the very least, the bishop is expected to ensure that priests have an adequate means of livelihood. There is anecdotal evidence that this is not always the case, particularly when priests have been dismissed from the clerical state. It has been proposed that bishops and religious superiors should endeavour to help priests who have abused to create worthwhile lives. This is consistent with the humanistic approach that is intrinsic to the Good Lives model.[21]

Dr Brendan Geary, the Provincial of the Marist Brothers' Province of West Central Europe who is also an author and a UK registered clinical psychologist, promotes the idea of 'Good Lives' for former clergy abusers. At the Boundary-breaking Colloquium on clergy sexual abuse held in January 2015 hosted by the University of Durham Centre for Catholic Studies, Dr Geary referred to the Good Lives model of treatment for sex offenders proposed by New Zealand clinical psychologist Professor Tony Ward in 2002 and since developed in various jurisdictions (http://www.goodlivesmodel.com/information). The Good Lives approach seeks to build therapy on the human strengths of the offender rather than focusing on deficits. It also begins from the premise that the offender has rights as a citizen and that helping the offender to have his needs met in a healthy, non-criminogenic way will be better for society while offering the offender the hope of a worthwhile life. While priests who have abused cannot return to pastoral ministry, there are other ways that they can serve the Church.

The Church, which is motivated by a theology of compassion and mercy, is well placed to create a supportive environment which with proper regard for safeguards, risk assessment and covenants of care, can establish programmes of best practice in the rehabilitation of offending priests. If the six priests whom I interviewed are representative of the priests in England and Wales and in the wider Catholic world, then such a programme would go a long way to assure them that brother priests who had abused would be cared for and offered the opportunity to build a better life.

Ending the silence

My position as insider researcher, although bringing benefits, could be argued to have drawbacks. Particular dynamics shaped the interview. They were brother priests, they were interviewed in their place of work or their home, and they knew my position as a brother priest, a researcher, a safeguarding co-ordinator, and a member of several strategy bodies for investigating child abuse. This inevitably impacted on what was said and not said within the interview, by both myself and the interviewees. The interviewees, for example, may have been likely to censor any responses that might have appeared critical of the Church's safeguarding activities or apportioned any blame to abuse victims themselves.

As a researcher and a brother priest, I was anxious as well neither to encourage nor fuel the notion that there is a direct correlation between celibacy and the abuse of minors, any more than there is a correlation between sexual orientation and the abuse of minors.

Generally, my insider status may have added to the ethical concerns that led me to decide against exploring or pursuing a number of areas of research. They include the following: whether any of the interviewees were themselves victims, whether they had any fantasies as regards the abuse of minors, their own experience of celibacy, and any exploration into their spiritual life. I chose not to explore any of these avenues because as a researcher I deemed them to be unnecessarily intrusive and inappropriate. I had to assume they were non-offending priests and I had to assume they were not victims. In my estimation, it would have been unethical to pursue lines of questioning about such conduct, guided as I was by the principles of beneficence and non-maleficence. The priests had agreed to be interviewed about the impact of abuse. I concluded that it would have lacked transparency in the research process to introduce more issues of a more personal nature.

On a further note, I think these areas of enquiry had the potential to fracture any possibility of a rich dialogue with these men which could produce the important data which did, in fact, emerge from the interviews. Also, if I had asked questions that invited priests to explore these areas, there would have been the risk of blurring the roles of researcher and therapist. My role at the time of the interviews was to be a researcher and to avoid, as far as possible, any further potential blurring of roles.

For me as the researcher, this thesis has unearthed several other possibilities for much needed research into the effects of the child sex abuse scandal on non-offending priests. The following areas perhaps warrant further exploration and research:

- ongoing human development training for priests especially around celibacy, loneliness, sexuality and intimacy;
- training in how to have difficult conversations about difficult subjects, and how to have conversations where there is an element of fear in the air;
- counselling to promote 'adult' relationships between bishops and priests;
- therapy or consultancy support for priests and bishops to create space to discuss how they have been affected by the abuse crisis;
- meetings of priests, with an independent facilitator, to enable the priests to talk to each other, listen to each other and engage with their bishop around these issues.

Equally, I became increasingly aware that there was, to a greater or lesser extent, a degree of disillusionment among the priests concerning their bishop or religious superior and exasperation that priests' voices seemed unheard. I believe the experience and perceptions of bishops and religious superiors also comprise an area that warrants serious research which would, for the first time to my knowledge, give voice to the bishops and religious superiors. I have recently begun a series of interviews with bishops and former bishops in the UK and Ireland to give them the same hearing that this study has given to priests.

Whilst conducting my interviews with the six priests I interviewed, it became clear to me as a researcher that no other issue had such an impact on them. My research found that nothing has contributed more powerfully to the vastly different way in which priests are now regarded both inside and outside the Roman Catholic Church than the crisis of child sexual abuse by a few of the clergy.

It is hard being a Catholic today; it is hard being a Catholic priest today. The crisis is such that in some circles priest and paedophile are still interchangeable words. We seem to have gone from one unhealthy view—'a priest would never do that'—to another equally unhealthy one—'he is a priest, so he probably did do that'. The following question in a letter in *The Weekend Australian* epitomizes this collapse in trust: 'Are there any parents with young children who still take them to church? If so, can they explain why?'[22] Such feelings are hard to accept for me both as a priest and as a counsellor.

I expect that the tragedy's full impact on both the institutional Church and how priests are regarded will only become clear in the years ahead. Some argue that there is nothing comparable to it in modern times. Story after story in the media has generated waves of numbness and bewilderment amongst priests and Catholics in general; this was reflected by all six interviewees. This point is further illustrated by a priest who wrote in a 1994 issue of *Commonweal*, a magazine on Catholicism, politics, and culture:

> Mixed with feelings of shame and embarrassment there is great anger. I am angry at the priest-pederasts and abusers ... If they knew what they were doing but could not control a compulsion to act out, then they were clearly sick. At this point they had two choices: to get professional help or to get out of the priesthood.[23]

As a researcher, one of the most valuable discoveries for me was to identify and detail the existence of a group of men, priests against whom accusations have not been made, whose needs have not previously been identified or catered for, as far as I am able to ascertain. I was satisfied that my qualitative approach produced such a valuable result.

I was left with the impression that, on the whole, priests have a deep and personal commitment to the priesthood. It seemed that this deep commitment sustained my six interviewees in most challenging times both to their individual priesthood and the brotherhood of the priests to which they belong. Whilst all of the interviewees have been severely shaken by the sexual abuse cases and the way that the bishops mishandled the situation, it seems that they remain priests because their commitment to the priesthood and to the Church is so integral to their ontology as priests.

The tension in being a researcher, a Roman Catholic priest and a counsellor was evident throughout this study, so much so that it was a topic of both concern and much debate during the vast majority of my sessions with my academic supervisors. Whilst this tension was fraught with difficulties, I am convinced it led to a greater depth of analysis and leant greater weight to the integrity of the data. As a non-offending Roman Catholic priest myself, I was interested to explore the view of other priests who were in my position but did not have the experience of being involved in this specialised field of work, nor the luxury of time to research the matter. Whilst I struggled at times to achieve the balance of being researcher, priest and counsellor, I am confident that the data presented is all the more valuable given the tension woven through the whole process.

This study supports the view that priests need to engage in research. The necessity of gaining more information about the priest population is primary to advancing the field.

This is the first piece of research that has invited non-offending priests to share their experience of the recent clerical sexual abuse crisis in England and Wales and beyond. There is a danger that there is only one area of narrative in the area of child sexual abuse—particularly clergy child sexual abuse—at the moment and that is the perspective of the victim. This is perfectly understandable, given how their voices were systemically not listened to in the past, either by the Church or society. However, this is not the only narrative—albeit a powerful one—which must be heard. The perspectives of non-offending priests must be added to the overall picture of the effects of the clerical child sexual abuse crisis even though they might not even be allowed to be considered as victims in the current climate. For them to claim victimhood—even secondary victimhood—might be perceived by some as selfish, uncaring, and another manifestation of clericalism.

This study might also contribute to reminding counsellors of the need to be constantly vigilant when listening to people who may not be perceived to be victims of abuse, or who do not present themselves as suffering individuals but who nonetheless carry wounds and burdens as a result of the behaviour of others. There are many people who carry burdens that often remain unrecognised and unheard and so become secondary victims whose lives are deeply affected by the behaviour of others. Their lives, identities, self-confidence, and well-being can be affected in a negative way, and there is seldom any attempt to reach out to them to listen to their needs, to understand how they have been affected and to attempt to alleviate their suffering. In this case, the group whose voices have been heard is a cohort of non-offending Roman Catholic priests who, to my knowledge, have until now suffered and have continued to minister in silence.

When it comes to the majority of people who feel unheard and unrecognised, the term 'elephant in the room' seems inadequate. For non-offending priests, at least, it seems that there is a whole herd of elephants. Perhaps this study will go some way to encouraging those in the field of counselling to be more proactive in reaching out to people in our communities who might well feel that they do not have a right to be heard. This was my experience with the interviewees for this thesis. Far from being unworthy of being heard, I am grateful to them for the rich data they shared which helped me to attempt to articulate the experiences and voices of those on the margins. The number of those on the margins could be a useful exercise for anybody working in the field of counselling and psychotherapy.

In recent years the voices of victims of sexual abuse have come to be heard and they can have a powerful say in how society responds to abuse. There are also therapists and researchers who dedicate their efforts to working with perpetrators. It could be a useful exercise for someone working in the field of counselling to attempt to quantify or at least name the other groups whose lives can be detrimentally affected by abuse and other traumatic events.

In the course of this research I am confident that I have identified the possibility that non-offending Catholic priests experience secondary victimhood with regards to the clerical child sexual abuse scandal. This is of course not only evident in the Catholic Church; other institutions and professions such as the BBC, education, social services, and the health service will no doubt have their fair share of secondary victims.

As an insider researcher I can testify that this subject matter has already been identified as an important contribution to knowledge within the Church. Since completing this study, I have been invited to share its findings at conferences across the United Kingdom, a European Safeguarding Conference in Luxembourg, as well as at symposia as far afield as Washington, Boston, Vancouver, and Peru. Also, in terms of counselling, this research can offer an important contribution in a range of ways: for example, there did not seem to exist any dynamic within the Church which would facilitate independent counselling for priests who felt unheard, somewhat disregarded and possibly discarded. For me, this whole process opened up that question and the possibilities of building bridges between two worlds, counselling and theology.

Reflecting back to that first interview with Matthew, this was what he seemed to be searching for as we spoke. 'Being authentically Catholic', he said, 'involves not splitting others off, not denying, not scapegoating.'

'How the hell did this happen?'

Notes

1   A. Ivereigh, *How to Defend the Faith without Raising Your Voice: Civil Responses to Catholic Hot-Button Issues* (Huntington, IN, USA: Our Sunday Visitor Publishing, 2012).

2   Quoted in *The Guardian*, 28 May 2015. The full statement is available from the Methodist Church at http://www.methodist.org.uk/news-and-events/news-releases/church-issues-%E2%80%98full-and-unreserved-apology%E2%80%99-to-abuse-survivors.

3   T. P. Doyle, 'Roman Catholic clericalism, religious duress, and clergy sexual abuse' in *Pastoral Psychology*, 51(3) (2003), pp. 189–231.

4   M. Keenan, *Child Sexual Abuse and the Catholic Church: Gender, Power, and Organizational Culture* (New York: Oxford University Press, 2011).

5   J. A. Weafer, *Thirty-three Good Men: Celibacy, Obedience and Identity. A Sociological Study of the Lived Experience of Irish Diocesan Priests in Modern Ireland, 1960-2010* (Dublin: The Columba Press, 2014), p. 159.

6   R. L. Rubens, *Fairbairn's structural theory*, available at: http://www.columbia.edu/~rr322/FAIRBAIRN.html, (2015).

7   D. Tindall, 'Policies and procedures for safeguarding children in the local Church' in *The Dark Night of the Catholic Church* (Stowmarket, SFK, UK: Kevin Mayhew, 2011), p. 550.

8   R. J. Neuhaus, 'In the aftermath of scandal', *First Things* February/2004, p. 60.

9   S. H. Louden and L. J. Francis, *The Naked Priest: What priests Really Think They're Doing* (London: Continuum, 2003).

10   See *The Sunday Times News Review*, 28 April 2002, p. 4.

11   C. Scicluna, 'Sexual abuse of children and young people by Catholic priests and religious: Description of the problem from a Church perspective' in *Proceedings of the Conference on Abuse of Children and Young People by Catholic Priests and Religious*, Vatican City, 2003. Libreria Editrice Vaticana, p. 13.

12   *Ibid.*, pp. 16-17.

13   *Ibid.*, p. 17.

14   B. Geary and J. M. Greer (eds), *The Dark Night of the Catholic Church* (Stowmarket, SFK, UK: Kevin Mayhew, 2011), p. 85.

15   Weafer, *Thirty-three Good Men*, p. 63.

16   Vatican II, *Christus Dominus*, 28.
17   E.Walsh, 'The relationship between bishop and priest', in *Priesthood Today: Ministry in a Changing Church* (Dublin: Veritas, 2014), pp. 275–283.
18   S. J. Rossetti, *Why Priests are Happy: A Study of the Psychological and Spiritual Health of Priests* (Notre Dame, IN, USA: Ave Maria Press, 2011), p. xiv.
19   A. M. Greeley, *Priests: A Calling in Crisis* (Chicago: The University of Chicago Press, 2004), pp. 6–10.
20   D. Mearns and B. Thorne, *Person-Centred Counselling in Action*, 4th edn, (London: Sage Publications, 1998 to 2013).
21   C. M. Chu and T. Ward, 'The good lives model of offender rehabilitation: Working positively with sexual offenders', in *Positive Criminology: The Good can Overcome the Bad* (Abingdon: Routledge, 2015), pp. 140–161.
22   See P. Day, 'Sexual abuse scandal forces a rethinking of Church. Crisis calls on all Catholics to be agents of change' in *La Croix* (2 June 2015).
23   See J. J. Dreese, 'The other victims of priest pedophilia: An inheritance squandered' in *Commonweal* 121/8 (April 1994) pp. 12.

Appendix

The Perception of Deans and Priests from a Catholic Diocese in Northern England October 2007

O N 31 August 2007 the bishop of the diocese wrote to his deans to invite them to a presentation and discussion at the Bishop's House about child protection policies and procedures. Individual anonymous questionnaires were also sent to all the clergy of the diocese. The meeting was held on 12 October 2007, with all deans present. The agenda included, among other child protection matters, a discussion of the questionnaire.

The chair of the Diocesan Child Protection Commission, a family law solicitor, first explained that the commission, consisting of people with a range of professional expertise, met approximately every two months. Cases that the child protection co-ordinator and the child protection advisor are concerned about are brought to the meeting for consideration and advice on how to proceed. The chair said he always reminded the commission that when considering a case the commission had a duty not only to the complainant or victim, but also the alleged perpetrator. It was therefore important that the evidence was weighed up properly, using the civil standard of proof, that is, the more unlikely the event the more cogent the evidence needs to be.

As the child protection co-ordinator, I reported that there had sometimes been a struggle with COPCA (Catholic Office for the Protection of Children and Vulnerable

Adults) especially when its timetable seemed too hurried and cumbersome, particularly in regard to Criminal Record Bureau (CRB) checks. [As recommended by the Church's 2007 Cumberlege Report, COPCA became the Catholic Safeguarding Advisory Service (CSAS); and, following Parliament's passage of the Protection of Freedoms Act 2012, the CRB became the Disclosure and Barring Service, a non-departmental public body of the United Kingdom government's Home Office.]

Feedback from the deans

I explained that I was attempting to get feedback from clergy about their thoughts on how child protection policies and procedures had affected their ministry. I then asked the deans to consider the questionnaire which had been sent to the clergy. The consultation process would include this discussion with the deans and obtaining feedback from the clergy. I then ran through the questionnaire briefly and asked for forthright responses, emphasising that all replies would be anonymous.

Some of the comments made by the deans at the meeting were as follows:

> In the current deanery where CRB is being implemented the people are very confident. It is giving them confidence for the future.

> I have heard in other dioceses that priests are suspended for a long length of time—the clergy are very apprehensive.

> There is a story going round the clergy that the diocese is going to request a copy of their passport, which they will send to all ports and airports if they ever get into trouble.

One dean admitted that he had been unaware of the commission's existence. Another complained that his parish child protection representative had not been properly trained because they could not answer the simplest of questions.

Some priests expressed concern that children had all the rights and they seemed to have none. The chair explained the paramountcy principle, adding it is not necessarily unequivocally accepted in all homes. In family law, the court is guided by the Children Act 1989 where the welfare of the child is the main consideration. There is a checklist. The child's wishes and feelings should be taken into consideration with the age and understanding of the child taken into account. A child's welfare should be of paramount consideration in the Church. It can cause difficulties—a balanced view is needed.

I explained that the paramountcy principle is necessary for the operation of the Church. The chair added that it permits adults to take control: 'The paramountcy principle refers primarily to the welfare not simply the rights of the child.'

I said it is mistakenly believed that the paramountcy principle means that the child should be believed and not the adult. The paramountcy principle allows for a child to be listened to and heard; there is no assumption of guilt or innocence during an initial disclosure.

At the end of the meeting, the deans were asked by the bishop to report the contents of the meeting back to their deanery conference later that month. All deans reported back and included written reports of comments made by the priests in their deaneries. Some of the comments are as follows:

> The approach of the Child Protection Commission sometimes seems cold, clinical and remote from

the practicalities of parish life ... It is time for us to move on to a system that is more proactive and encouraging, where priests and lay volunteers are supported in their ministry to young and vulnerable people ... It was agreed that CSAS (despite its name) would be more in tune with the realities of parish life and would give encouragement to all who see their work with children as part of the mission of the Church. We need to be able to move on with confidence whilst still being vigilant about the welfare of children.

We are greatly encouraged especially in the contrast to the aftermath of the Nolan Report ... The people in the parish are far more confident these days.

It was useful to discuss the difference between the child being 'listened to' and the child being 'believed'.

I am pleased to hear that no priest has been abandoned in this diocese; but that needs to be made clear to everyone with details in writing.

Child protection is having a negative effect on ourselves and our volunteers. Are we being treated as guilty until proven guilty? Everyone should feel that they are respected and treated fairly.

At one deanery:

There was much discussion of possible reaction of ecclesiastical authorities to anonymous accusations. There was anxiety about the perception that clergy might be seen as guilty until proved innocent. Instances were quoted (not from this diocese) where that had indeed been the case. It would seem that this is the only instance where presumption of guilt prevails—in other crimes the accused is presumed innocent until proved guilty.

At another:

> Unfounded allegations: Concern was expressed as
> to how such allegations would be perceived: 'no
> smoke without fire'. How might an individual cope
> facing such a situation? Some have left their par-
> ishes without any instruction to do so; but the
> feeling was that this was not the best course to take.
> It was reported that all allegations to date in this
> diocese have been handled sensitively and justly;
> but it was also recognised that the person would
> still feel 'damaged'.
>
> How would someone expect to be treated if an
> allegation were made? Those present felt strongly
> that the bishop and the child protection co-ordinator
> would be supportive, although concern was
> expressed as to whether this would be the case from
> all members of the commission.

One deanery reported that after putting it to a vote it was
unanimously agreed that some members of the commission come across as anti-clerical and therefore unap-
proachable.

Another deanery:

> In light of the discussion about the various 'bal-
> ances' sought (balance of evidence, balance of
> probabilities, balance of justice for one making an
> allegation and one against whom it is made, et
> cetera), it was considered important that we have
> a 'balance of attitude' towards the issues.

Another deanery:

1. Comments on COPCA (Catholic Office for the Protection of Children and Vulnerable Adults) over the past five
   years:

   Structures set up by COPCA: though useful, seemed
   over-bureaucratic and had an over-critical approach, such

as the principle that anyone accused should be treated as innocent until proved guilty was not honoured. The Catholic culture was not sufficiently appreciated.

As put into practice by the diocesan Child Protection Commission: there were several comments: unease about some personnel's approach: seemed to be somewhat aggressive and condescending; lack of respect for priests, most of whom are long-serving in trustworthy positions of a high degree.

Time for a personality change as with COPCA: there was general appreciation of the diligence and support of the commission's co-ordinator.

2. How might CSAS be integrated into the Church family in England and Wales?

a) As a more sensitive and respectful liaison with clergy.

a) As a Christocentric service, in line with everything else in the life of the Church. (This would contrast with the 'social service' type of approach of COPCA, lacking the inspiration of Christian love—which does not exclude clarity of procedure, a wholesome approach, efficiency or accountability.)

Individual questionnaires for the clergy

From the hundreds of questionnaires sent out, 45.5% were completed and returned. The priests responding to the questionnaire fell into the following five age ranges: 15% were aged 30 to 40; 15% were aged 40 to 50; 22% were aged 50 to 60; 30% were aged 60 to 70; and 18% were aged 70 to 80. There were no priests in this particular diocese in the 20 to 30 age group. Some replies came back with anonymous written comments which are included below after the question to which they refer.

As the researcher, I was very surprised that the priests in the age group 70 to 80 were unanimous in their support for the child protection policies. I had wrongly assumed that this age group would be the most resistant. Those aged 60 to 70 expressed the most concern and reported the majority of negative comments.

Question 1

Have the policies and procedures adopted by the diocese affected your ministry with children and vulnerable adults?
Answers: a little, 52%; a lot, 28%; not at all, 20%.

Question 2

Do you think these changes are: positive, negative, a mixture or neutral?
Answers: a mixture, 47%; positive, 39%; negative, 7%; neutral, 7%.

Question 3

The Child Protection Commission has striven to be a resource to the bishop, priests and people of the diocese. How successful has it been in attempting to achieve this goal?
Answers: always, 59%; occasionally, 34%; not at all, 7%.
Comments:

> I think that some policies adopted have in fact made work with young people more difficult. I know we must strive always for prevention and protection; but our priority must always be the Gospel. Have we asked: 'Are the policies we adopt helping promote the Gospel?' I would also like clarification regarding canon law. Ignoring this issue won't make it go away. Each priest must clearly know where they stand!

> 1. The bureaucracy can be very burdensome, especially when people have to apply for multiple CRB checks.

2. The attitudes adopted by the (lay) staff of the commission can sometimes appear aggressive, insulting and bullying.

3. On the only occasion I was involved with someone asking advice from the commission on a protection matter, I was very impressed by the professionalism displayed.

The COPCA approach was very clinical. Correct structures appeared to be all that mattered. Rightly or wrongly, it left some priests fearful that unknowingly or unwittingly they could fall foul of the law. As the accused they would have no rights and little if any support—a life-long vocation would be thrown on the rubbish heap.

I feel that the COPCA approach was necessary; but it is time to move on. We need to reclaim the mission of the Church to the young and vulnerable, and to re-establish our involvement as priests in that ministry.

I've been very glad of the commission's help on a number of occasions. It's been invaluable.

Question 4

The parish child protection reps are in place to be a resource to the parish priest and the parishioners. Do you regard your parish rep as a valuable resource?

Answers: always, 59%; occasionally, 34%; not at all, 7%.

Question 5

Would you feel confident to approach the Child Protection Commission if you had any issues around children and vulnerable adults?

Answers: always, 50%; occasionally, 31%; not at all, 19%.

Comments:

The legal presumption of innocence does not seem to be operative in cases of false allegations, and is a serious omission.

Because of the high profile that child protection issues have in the Church, it affects ministry in that now you always have to think about ensuring EVERYONE is safe—children, volunteers, vulnerable people, and yourself as well.

Much good has been done with regard to procedures and guidelines but clergy fears over allegations (false or unproven) are still very real. Clergy are not sure of what provision is made in such circumstances but assume that the same agency that would investigate disclosures/allegations would also support them: is there a clash of interest here? Thanks for all your endeavours.

The introduction of the commission I am sure has been for the best. But it has been said that priests who have been accused have been treated rather badly. I am not sure if the commission could react to an allegation coolly and measured. It seems rather that (and this is the only case in British law) you are guilty until proven innocent. There have been many such cases around the country—including within our own diocese where priests have been treated almost with disdain when there is no case against them.

It has also been said that priests are very vulnerable insomuch as the diocese would react in the negative rather than the positive and would not pay for the cost of a barrister in such cases—cited as being too expensive.

All these issues have been discussed in the National Council of Priests, but I still have no evidence that anything has been done to alleviate the worry of priests across the board.

Question 6

If you found yourself the subject of an allegation are you confident that the Child Protection Commission would treat you fairly and with respect?

Answers: yes, 43%; not sure, 26%; don't know, 17%; no, 14%.

Comments:

> Once falsely accused, a priest could never prove his innocence.

> I'm not sure I would have answered question 6 so positively if I was not aware of how the commission has dealt with someone I know. I would probably have opted for "not sure" or "don't know". So if these are the main responses to that question it is probably because most people have not had any direct dealings with the commission.

> All animals are equal. Some are more equal than others.

> While the so-called paramountcy principle is maintained, justice will never happen or be seen to happen. It conflicts with the human rights of clergy and defies canon law. It is also possibly illegal as it discriminates on the ground of age.

Question 7

Has the adoption of child protection policies and procedures given you confidence to continue your ministry with children and vulnerable adults?

Answers: yes, 54%; not sure, 32%; no, 8%; don't know, 6%.

Comments:

Credence must rightly be given to children—no problem—but not at the expense of denying other persons respect of their rights.

Two wrongs do not make a right. Not to listen to a child is wrong—and we need to create the situation where a child can freely speak knowing he or she will be listened to. But to exaggerate that to exclude fairness and impartiality to others is wrong—and that is what seems to be happening. Justice has to be seen to happen even-handedly and fairly.

Bibliography

Church documents

Bishops' Conference of England and Wales, *Directory on the Canonical Status of the Clergy: Rights Obligations and Procedures*. London: Catholic Truth Society, 2009.

Catholic Safeguarding Advisory Service, 'Review of Congregation for the Doctrine of the Faith'. In: *Safeguarding Coordinators and Officers Meeting, Swanwick* (9 February 2009).

Coleridge, M. 'Seeing the faces, hearing the voices', *Pentecost Letter on Sexual Abuse of the Young in the Catholic Church, 23 May 2010*. Canberra: Archdiocese of Canberra and Goulburn, 2010.

Congregation for the Doctrine of the Faith, Circular Letter to Assist Episcopal Conferences on *Developing Guidelines for Dealing with Cases of Sexual Abuse of Minors Perpetrated by Clerics* (2011).

Cumberlege Commission, *Safeguarding With Confidence: Keeping Children and Vulnerable Adults Safe in the Catholic Church*. London: Incorporated Catholic Truth Society, 2007.

Diocese of Salford, *Parish Safeguarding Representatives Training Material*. Salford: Roman Catholic Diocese of Salford, 2002–2015.

Scicluna, C. An address to a conference on abuse of children and young people: *Sexual Abuse of Children and Young People by Catholic Priests and Religious: Description of the Problem from a Church Perspective*. Vatican City: Libreria Editrice Vaticana, 2–5 April 2003, pp. 13–23.

Books

Adler, P. A. and Adler, P. *Membership Roles in Field Research*. London: Sage, 1987.

Adler, P., et al. *The Oxford Handbook of Sociology, Social Theory and Organization Studies: Contemporary Currents.* Oxford: Oxford University, 1990.

Allegations Management Advisers, *Guidance for Safer Working Practice for Adults who Work With Children and Young People.* London: UK Department for Children, Schools and Families, 2007.

Bates, B. F. *The Institute of Charity: Rosminians, Their Irish Story 1860–2003.* Dublin: Ashfield, 2003.

Bradshaw, J. *Healing the Shame that Binds You,* revised edn. Deerfield Beach, FL: Health Communications, 2005.

Brinkmann, S. and Kvale, S. 'Ethics in Qualitative Psychological Research'. In: C. Willig and W. Stainton-Rogers (eds.), *The Sage Handbook of Qualitative Research in Psychology.* London: Sage, 2008.

Chinnici, J. *When Values Collide.* Berkeley, CA: Orbis, 2010.

Chu, C. M. and Ward, T. 'The Good Lives Model of Offender Rehabilitation: Working Positively with Sexual Offenders'. In: H. Ronel and D. Segev (eds.), *Positive Criminology: The Good Can Overcome the Bad.* Abingdon: Routledge, 2015.

Conway, E. (ed.) *Priesthood Today: Ministry in a Changing Church.* Dublin: Veritas, 2014.

Cozzens, D. B. *The Changing Face of the Priesthood.* Collegeville, MN: Liturgical, 2000.

Denzin, N. K. and Lincoln, Y. S. *The Sage Handbook of Qualitative Research,* 4th edn. London: Sage, 2011.

Doyle, T. P., Sipe, A. W. R. and Wall, P. J. *Sex, Priests, and Secret Codes: The Catholic Church's 2,000-Year Paper Trail of Sexual Abuse.* Los Angeles: Volt, 2005.

Flowers, P. and Shaw, R. *Expanding the Evidence within Evidence-Based Healthcare: Thinking about the Context, Acceptability and Feasibility of Interventions.* Birmingham: Aston University, 2010.

Furet, J.-B. *The Life of Joseph-Benoît Marcellin Champagnat, 1789–1840.* Rome: Marist Brothers, 1856.

Galloway, K. and Gamble, D. *Time for Action: Sexual Abuse, the Churches and a New Dawn for Survivors.* London: Churches Together in Britain and Ireland, 2002.

Geary, B. and Greer, J. M. (eds.) *The Dark Night of the Catholic Church.* Stowmarket: Kevin Mayhew, 2011.

Goode, H., McGee, H. and O'Boyle, C. *Time to Listen: Confronting Child Sexual Abuse by Catholic Clergy in Ireland.* Dublin: Liffey, 2003.

Greeley, A. M. *Priests: A Calling in Crisis.* Chicago: University of Chicago, 2004.

Greer, J. M. *Protecting Your Child from Sexual Abuse.* Stowmarket: Kevin Mayhew, 2011.

Greer, J. M. *Child Sexual Abuse: Addressing Concerns in Ministries to Children and Adolescents.* Stowmarket: Kevin Mayhew, 2012.

Gubi, P. M. *Listening to Less-Heard Voices: Developing Counsellors' Awareness.* Chester: University of Chester, 2015.

Gubi, P. M. (ed.) *Spiritual Accompaniment and Counselling: Journeying with Psyche and Soul.* Philadelphia: Jessica Kingsley, 2015.

Gutierrez, G. *A Theology of Liberation: History, Politics, and Salvation.* Maryknoll, NY: Orbis, 1973.

Haywood, T. W. and Green, J. 'Cleric Serial Offenders: Clinical Characteristics and Treatment Approaches'. In: L. B. Schlesinger (ed.), *Serial Offenders: Current Thought, Recent Findings.* Boca Raton, FL: CRC, 2000.

Heidegger, M. *Being and Time,* translated by J. Macquarrie and E. Robinson. Oxford: Blackwell 1927/1962.

Ivereigh, A. *How to Defend the Faith Without Raising Your Voice: Civil Responses to Catholic Hot-Button Issues.* Huntington, IN: Our Sunday Visitor, 2012.

Jenkins, P. *The New Anti-Catholicism: The Last Acceptable Prejudice*. Oxford: Oxford University, 2003.

Keenan, M. *Child Sexual Abuse and the Catholic Church: Gender, Power, and Organizational Culture*. New York: Oxford University, 2011.

Kvale, S. *Doing Interviews*, vol. 2 of *The Sage Qualitative Research Kit*. London: Sage, 2007.

Laing, R. D. *The Divided Self: An Existential Study in Sanity and Madness*. London: Tavistock, 1960.

Littleton, J. and Maher, E. (eds.). *What Being a Catholic Means to Me*. Dublin: Columba, 2009.

Louden, S. H. and Francis, L. J. *The Naked Priest: What Priests Really Think They're Doing*. London: Continuum, 2003.

Manchester Safeguarding Children Board. *Safeguarding Children Procedures*. Manchester: MSCB, 2007.

McLeod, J. *Qualitative Research in Counselling and Psychotherapy*, 1st edn. London: Sage, 2001.

Mearns, D. and Thorne, B. *Person-Centred Counselling in Action*, 4th edn. London: Sage, 2013.

O'Brien, B. 'Shattered Assumptions: A Tale of Two Traumas'. In: E. Maher and E. O'Brien (eds.), *From Prosperity to Austerity*. Manchester: Manchester University, 2014.

Parry, K. *Towards a Culture of Safeguarding*. London: National Catholic Safeguarding Commission, 2012.

Plante, T. G. (ed.). *Bless Me Father For I Have Sinned: Perspectives on Sexual Abuse Committed by Roman Catholic Priests*. Westport, CT: Praeger, 1999.

Plante, T. and McChesney, K. *Sexual Abuse in the Catholic Church: A Decade of Crisis 2002–2012*. Santa Barbara, CA: Praeger, 2011.

Richardson, W. *The Presumption of Innocence in Canonical Trials of Clerics Accused of Child Sexual Abuse.* Louvain: Peeters, 2011.

Rorty, R. *Philosophy and the Mirror of Nature.* Princeton, NJ: Princeton University, 1979.

Rossetti, S. J. *Slayer of the Soul: Child Sexual Abuse and the Catholic Church.* New London, CT: Twenty-third, 1990.

Rossetti, S. J. *Why Priests Are Happy: A Study of the Psychological and Spiritual Health of Priests.* Notre Dame, IN: Ave Maria, 2011.

Seewald, P. *Benedict XVI: An Intimate Portrait.* San Francisco: Ignatius, 2008.

Sipe, R. *Celibacy in Crisis: A Secret World Revisited.* Hove: Brunner-Routledge, 2003.

Smith, J. A. *Interpretative Phenomenological Analysis.* London: Birkbeck, 2007.

Smith, J. A. (ed.) *Qualitative Psychology: A Practical Guide to Research Methods.* 2nd ed. London: Sage, 2008.

Smith, J. A., Jarman, M. and Osborn, M. 'Doing Interpretative Phenomenological Analysis'. In: M. Murray and K. Chamberlain (eds.), *Qualitative Health Psychology: Theories and Methods.* London: Sage, 1999.

Smith, J. A., Flowers, P. and Larkin, M. *Interpretative Phenomenological Analysis: Theory, Method and Research.* London: Sage, 2009.

Swinton, J. and Mowat, H. *Practical Theology and Qualitative Research.* London: SCM, 2006.

Tangney, J. P. 'Self-Relevant Emotions'. In: M. R. Leary and J. P. Tangney (eds.), *Handbook of Self and Identity.* New York: Guilford, 2003.

Walsh, E. 'The Relationship between Bishop and Priest'. In: E. Conway (ed.) *Priesthood Today: Ministry in a Changing Church.* Dublin: Veritas, 2014.

Weafer, J. A. *Thirty-Three Good Men: Celibacy, Obedience and Identity*: A *Sociological Study of the Lived Experience of Irish Diocesan Priests in Modern Ireland, 1960–2010.* Dublin: Columba, 2014.

Werdel, M. B. and Wicks, R. J. *Primer on Posttraumatic Growth: An Introduction and Guide.* Hoboken, NJ: John Wiley, 2012.

Worden, J. W. *Grief Counselling and Grief Therapy: A Handbook for the Mental Health Practitioner.* 1st ed. London: Tavistock, 1983; 4th ed. Hove: Routledge, 2010.

Articles

Asselin, M. 'Insider Research: Issues to Consider when Doing Qualitative Research in Your Own Setting'. In: *Journal for Nurses in Professional Development* 19/2 (2003), pp. 99–103.

Brannick, T. and Coghlan, D. 'In Defence of Being Native: The Case for Insider Academic Research'. In: *Organizational Research Methods* 10/1 (2007), pp. 59–74.

Brenneis, M. J. 'Personality Characteristics of Clergy and of Psychologically "Impaired" Clergy'. In: *American Journal of Pastoral Counseling* 4/2 (2001), pp. 17–30.

Campbell, F. 'The Catholic Church and the British Government'. In: *Magnificat: Liturgies and Events of the Papal Visit of Pope Benedict XVI to the United Kingdom.* London: Catholic Church, 2010.

Christie, J. 'When Theology Trumps Psychology'. In: *The Tablet* (15 February 2014), pp. 14–17.

Cozzens, D. B. 'The Priest's Crisis of Soul: 3'. In: *The Tablet* (5 August 2000), p. 8.

Dorr, D. 'Sexual Abuse and Spiritual Abuse'. In: *The Furrow* 51/10 (2000), pp. 523–531.

Doyle, T. P. 'Roman Catholic Clericalism, Religious Duress, and Clergy Sexual Abuse'. In: *Pastoral Psychology* 51/3 (2003), pp. 189–231.

Doyle, T. P. 'Clericalism: Enabler of Clergy Sexual Abuse'. In: *Pastoral Psychology* 54/3 (2006), pp. 189–213.

Doyle, T. P. 'The Spiritual Trauma Experienced by Victims of Sexual Abuse by Catholic Clergy'. In: *Pastoral Psychology* 58/3 (2009), pp. 239–260.

Elliot, R., Fischer, C. T. and Rennie, D. L. 'Evolving Guidelines for Publication of Qualitative Research Studies in Psychological and Related Fields'. In: *British Journal of Clinical Psychology* 38/3 (1999), pp. 215–229.

Farrell, D. P. 'Sexual Abuse Perpetrated by Roman Catholic Priests'. In: *Mental Health, Religion & Culture* 12/1 (2009), pp. 39–53.

Francis, P. C. and Turner, N. R. 'Sexual Misconduct within the Christian Church: Who are the Perpetrators and those they Victimize?' In: *Counselling and Values* 39/3 (1995), pp. 218–227.

Fredrickson, B. 'The Role of Positive Emotions in Positive Psychology'. In: *The American Psychologist* 56/3 (2001), pp. 218–226.

Goldner, V. 'The Sexual Abuse Crisis and the Catholic Church: Gender, Sexuality, Power and Discourse'. In: *Studies in Gender and Sexuality* 5/1 (2004), pp. 1–9.

Greeley, A. M. 'How Serious is the Problem of Sexual Abuse by Clergy?' In: *America* 168/10 (1993), pp. 6–10.

Hudson, P. E. 'Spirituality as a Component in a Treatment Programme for Sexually Addicted Roman Catholic Clergy'. In: *Counselling and Values* 41/2 (1997), pp. 174–182.

Keenan, M. 'Child Sexual Abuse: The Heart of the Matter'. In: *The Furrow* 53/11 (2002), pp. 597–605.

Keenan, M. 'The Institution and the Individual: Child Sexual Abuse by Clergy'. In: *The Furrow* 57/1 (2006), pp. 3–8.

Keenan, M. 'Researching the Lives of Irish Roman Catholic Clergy Who have Sexually Abused Minors: Collaborative

Inquiry'. In: *Qualitative Social Work* 11/3 (2012), pp. 282–298.

McCall, D. 'Sex and the Clergy'. In: *Sexual Addiction and Compulsivity* 9/2–3 (2002), pp. 81–95.

McGlone, G. 'Prevalence and Incidence of Roman Catholic Clerical Sex Offenders'. In: *Sexual Addiction and Compulsivity* 10/2–3 (2003), pp. 111–121.

Neuhaus, R. J. 'In the Aftermath of Scandal'. In: *First Things* February 2004, pp. 58–76.

O'Donohue, J. 'Before the Dawn I Begot You'. In: *The Furrow* 57/9 (2006), pp. 463–473.

Reid, K., Flowers, P., and Larkin M. 'Exploring Lived Experience'. In: *The Psychologist* 18/1 (2005), pp. 20–23.

Robertson, C. 'In Pursuit of Life Histories: The Problem of Bias'. In: *Frontiers: A Journal of Women Studies* 7(2) (1983), pp.63–69.

Saffiotti, L. M. 'Fostering/Hindering Christian Maturity'. In: *Human Development* 26/3 (2005), pp. 30–36.

Saradjian, A. and Nobus, D. 'Cognitive Distortions of Religious Professionals Who Sexually Abuse Children'. In: *Journal of Interpersonal Violence* 18(8) (2003), pp. 905–923.

Shulman, L. 'Learning to Talk About Taboo Subjects: A Lifelong Professional Challenge' In: *Social Work with Groups* 25/1–2 (2003), pp. 139–150.

Smith, J. A. 'Beyond the Divide between Cognition and Discourse: Using Interpretative Phenomenological Analysis in Health Psychology'. In: *Psychology & Health* 11/2 (1996), pp. 261–271.

Smith, J. A. 'Reflecting on the Development of Interpretative Phenomenological Analysis and its Contribution to Qualitative Research in Psychology'. In: *Qualitative Research in Psychology* 1/1 (2004), pp. 39–54.

Smyth, D. 'The Land of the Pirates: Clerical Culture and Sexual Abuse'. In: *The Furrow* 60/9 (2009), pp. 471–474.

Terry, K. J. 'Stained Glass: The Nature and Scope of Child Sexual Abuse in the Catholic Church'. In: *Criminal Justice and Behavior* 35/5 (2008), pp. 549–569.

Ward, T. 'Good Lives and the Rehabilitation of Offenders: Promises and Problems', *Aggression and Violent Behavior* 7 (2002), pp. 513–528.

Yardley, L. 'Dilemmas in Qualitative Health Research'. In: *Psychology and Health* 15/2 (2000), pp. 215–228.

Theses

McGlone, G. Abstract of dissertation *Sexually Offending and Non-Offending Roman Catholic Priests: Characterization and Analysis.* San Diego, CA: Alliant International University, 2001.

Morgan, E. Unpublished thesis *Canon 384: Relationship between the Bishop and His Priests.* Louvain-la-Neuve: University of Louvain, 2014.

Reports

Beal, J. Presentation at a Catholic University of America Canon Law Conference. Washington, DC: July 2004.

Catholic Safeguarding Advisory Service. *Annual Report.* London: Catholic Trust for England and Wales, 2014.

Child Exploitation and Online Protection Command Academy, Numerous documents and reports. London: National Crime Agency, n.d.

Children, Schools and Families Committee, *Allegations against School Staff, 5ᵗʰ Report of the House of Commons Committee 2008–2009.* London: The Stationery Office Limited, House of Commons, 2009.

Children, Schools and Families Committee, *Sure Start Children's Centres. 5ᵗʰ Report of the House of Commons Committee 2009–2010*. London: The Stationery Office Limited, House of Commons, 2010.

Greer, J. M. A paper prepared for a Safeguarding Children and Young People Conference: *Secondary Victims in a Sexual Abuse Scandal*. Rome: Marist Brothers General House, 21–28 March 2012.

Hanson, R. K., Pfafflin, F. and Lutz, M. (eds.). A report prepared for a conference on the abuse of children and young people by Catholic priests and religious: *Sexual Abuse in the Catholic Church: Scientific and Legal Perspectives*. Vatican City: Libreria Editrice Vaticana, 2–5 April 2003.

Mellor, L. and Sachs, J. A paper presented to a conference on: *Child Panic and Child Protection Policy: A Critical Examination of Policies from New South Wales and Queensland*. Auckland: Educational Research, Risks and Dilemmas Joint Annual Conference of the Australian and New Zealand Associations for Research in Education, 29 November—3 December 2003.

Office for Standards in Education, Children's Services and Skills, *Briefing for Section 5 Inspectors on Safeguarding Children*. Manchester: Ofsted, 2009.

O'Sullivan, B. and Geary, B. A paper prepared for a Marist conference: *What Have We Learned About Brothers and Priests Who Abuse Children*. Rome: International Conference for Marist Provincials, June 2012.

Terry, K., et al. *The Causes and Context of Sexual Abuse of Minors by Catholic Priests in the United States, 1950–2010: A Report Presented to the United States Conference of Catholic Bishops by the John Jay College Research Team*. Washington, DC: United States Conference of Catholic Bishops, 2011.

Working Party of the Canon Law Society of Great Britain and Ireland. *Responding to Allegations of Clerical Child Abuse:*

Recommendations for Harmonising the Nolan Report and the Code of Canon Law. Ayr: Canon Law Society of Great Britain and Ireland, 2004.

Proceedings

Anon. Summary of the Anglophone Conference for Safeguarding. (n.d. 2008) Rome: Roman Catholic Church, 2008.

Electronic documents

Allen, J. L. R., Jr. 'Is Vatican Letter on Abuse a "Smoking Gun"?' In: *National Catholic Reporter* (19 January 2011). <http://ncronline.org/blogs/ncr-today/vatican-letter-abuse-smoking-gun> [accessed 5 August 2014].

Australia. Royal Commission into Institutional Responses to Child Sexual Abuse. *Commission Website* (n.d. 2014). <http://www.childabuseroyalcommission.gov.au/> [accessed 29 May 2015].

Callaghan, B. 'On Scandal and Scandals'. In: *Thinking Faith* (13 April 2010). <http://www.thinkingfaith.org/articles/20100415_1.htm.> [accessed 20 July 2014].

Church of England. *Safeguarding.* (n.d. 2015). <https://www.churchofengland.org/clergy-office-holders/protecting-and-safeguarding-children-and-adults-who-are-vulnerable.aspx> [accessed 27 May 2015].

Commonwealth of Massachusetts Legislature. *An Act Requiring Certain Religious Officials to Report Abuse of Children.* Boston, MA: Commonwealth of Massachusetts, 2002. <https://malegislature.gov/Laws/SessionLaws/Acts/2002/Chapter107> [accessed 12 June 2015].

Cook, C. J. and Guertin, C. L. 'How Childhood Sexual Abuse Affects Adult Survivors' Images of God: A Resource for Pastoral Helpers'. In: *Sacred Spaces* 2 (2010), pp. 38–55. <http://www.aapc.org/media/47481/cookguertin.pdf> [accessed 18 September 2014].

Day, P. 'Australian Catholics Humiliated by the Sins of the Fathers'. In: *The Tablet* (3 June 2015). <http://www.thetablet.co.uk/blogs/1/659/-australian-catholics-humiliated-by-the-sins-of-the-fathers> [accessed 10 June 2015].

Jenkins, P. (1996). *The Uses of Clerical Scandal*. Institute on Religion and Public Life (February 1996). <http://www.firstthings.com/article/1996/02/004-the-uses-of-clerical-scandal> [accessed 19 September 2014].

Methodist Church Past Cases Review. *Courage, Cost and Hope* (April 2015). <http://www.methodist.org.uk/media/1683823 /past-cases-review-2013–2015-final.pdf> [accessed 1 June 2015].

Peterson, M. R., Mouton, R. and Doyle, T. P. *The Problem of Sexual Molestation by Roman Catholic Clergy: Meeting the Problem in a Comprehensive and Responsible Manner.* A then-confidential (June 1985) manual for American Roman Catholic bishops later published online (n.d.). <http://www.bishop-accountability.org/reports/ 1985_06_09_Doyle_Manual/#forward> [accessed 8 October 2014].

Murphy Commission of Investigation. *Report into the Catholic Archdiocese of Dublin.* (n.d. 2009). <http://www.justice.ie/en /JELR/Pages/PB09000504> [accessed 6 September 2014].

Nolan Committee. *The Final Report* (2001). Cumberlege Commission (n.d.). <http://www.cathcom.org/mysharedaccounts /cumberlege/finalnolan1.htm> [accessed 14 July 2014].

O'Brien, B. '"Mental Reservation" and the Church's Version of Truth'. In: *The Irish Times* (28 November 2009). <http://www.irishtimes.com/opinion/mental-reservation-and-the-church-s-version-of-truth-1.780422> [accessed 26 November 2014].

Rubens, R. L. *Fairbairn's Structural Theory.* New York: Columbia University, n.d. <http://www.columbia.edu/ ~rr322/FAIRBAIRN.html> [accessed 28 April 2015].

Ryan Commission to Inquire into Child Abuse. *The Commission Final Report* (n.d. 2009). <http://www.childabusecommission.ie/rpt/> [accessed 4 August 2014].

Scotland. Child Protection Improvement Programme. *Child Protection* (n.d.). <http://www.gov.scot/Topics/People/Young-People/protecting/child-protection> [accessed 17 May 2015].

Smith, J. A. 'Evaluating the Contribution of Interpretative Phenomenological Analysis'. *Health Psychology Review*, 5(1) (2011), pp. 9–27. <http://dx.doi.org/10.1080/17437199.2010.510659> [accessed 22 October 2015].

United Kingdom. Disclosure and Barring Service. *Disclosure and Barring Service* (n.d.). <https://www.gov.uk/government/organisations/disclosure-and-barring-service> [accessed 3 December 2014].

Lightning Source UK Ltd.
Milton Keynes UK
UKHW03f0031250418
321526UK00001B/6/P

9 780852 448410